WOVEN & QUILTED

That Patchwork Place®

MARY ANNE CAPLINGER

CREDITS

Editor-in-Chief............................ Barbara Weiland
Technical Editor .... Christine Barnes
Managing Editor .... Greg Sharp
Copy Editor .... Liz McGehee
Proofreaders .... Tina Cook, Leslie Phillips
Illustrator .... Brian Metz
Photographer .... Brent Kane
Design Director .... Judy Petry
Text and Cover Designer .... Amy Shayne
Design Assistant .... Claudia L'Heureux

MISSION STATEMENT

WE ARE DEDICATED TO PROVIDING QUALITY PRODUCTS THAT
ENCOURAGE CREATIVITY AND PROMOTE SELF-ESTEEM IN OUR
CUSTOMERS AND OUR EMPLOYEES.

WE STRIVE TO MAKE A DIFFERENCE
IN THE LIVES WE TOUCH.

That Patchwork Place is an employee-owned, financially secure company.

DEDICATION

To John, for continued love and support through all my deadlines.

ACKNOWLEDGMENTS

Special thanks to:

John, our children Mike and Julie, and our friend Joan Jacobs Gaylord as they keep pushing this "non-techie" into the world of word processing and diagramming on the computer;

All my students over the years who have been so encouraging and receptive to new ideas;

Fran Ginthwain and Karen James Swing, who contributed their work to this book;

Melissa Birdsong, for help with diagramming, layout, fabric selection, and general brainstorming;

Kathryn Faille, for proofreading the basic directions;

Christine Barnes, for careful and always cheerful editing;

That Patchwork Place, especially Barbara Weiland, for the opportunity to write this book.

Woven and Quilted
© 1995 by Mary Anne Caplinger
That Patchwork Place, Inc., PO Box 118
Bothell, WA 98041-0118 USA

Library of Congress Cataloging-in-Publication Data
Caplinger, Mary Anne
    Woven and quilted / Mary Anne Caplinger.
        p.   cm.
    ISBN 1-56477-091-5
    1. Machine quilting—Patterns. 2. Strip quilting—Patterns.
    3. Hand weaving. 4. Quilted goods. I. Title.
TT835.C368 1995
746.46—dc20   94-23571
                                                        CIP

Printed in Hong Kong
00 99 98 97 96 95 6 5 4 3 2 1

TABLE OF CONTENTS

PREFACE

Fun! Joy in the process! That's what was missing. As I bent over my sewing machine, frowning, teeth clenched, carefully sewing together yet another row of 1" squares so they would meet at the corners, I realized that I was hopelessly frustrated. I was ripping as much as I was sewing. The seam lines of those twelve little squares would not line up. Other quilters pieced hundreds of small triangles and hexagons, and their points matched. They seemed to enjoy that kind of work. I'd been sewing for more than thirty years—why couldn't I do it? More important, why didn't I like doing it?

I had to admit that traditional piecing was too tedious for me. What a revelation! After years of sewing tailored suits and coats and doing intricate hand and machine embroidery, I could not easily and accurately sew twelve little squares together. There had to be a way to get the look I wanted from a process that was enjoyable. It was up to me to find it.

The woven and quilted technique described in this book is the result of that search for a satisfying union of process and effect. I began by listing three goals: soft edges, small bits of color scattered across the surface, and a working method to replace precision piecing (what heresy!). The first two, soft edges and mottled colors, came from my love of French Impressionist paintings. The sketchy shapes, the splashes of color, and the off-center focus that typify Impressionism have been a continual source of inspiration to me. I was looking for my own way to express these concepts.

One of my friends had a color study of woven construction paper hanging in her sewing room. Sitting there, waiting for her to finish a phone call, I looked at that small weaving and thought, I wonder if I could do that with fabric? As it turned out, it could be done. I began cutting and weaving printed stationery and origami papers, then experimented with plain and printed cotton, silk, and knit fabrics. Once I got started, I found inspiration for new pieces everywhere I looked.

That was many years ago, and I'm still tearing and weaving fabrics and enjoying it immensely. It's proven to be an effective way to get that blend of small shapes and soft edges that I'd been trying for. Of course, there are still parts of the process that are tedious, but I'm learning to think of them as "meditation time." The results are most certainly worth the effort.

I hope you'll try weaving with fabrics and discover, as I did, the intriguing possibilities. The woven and quilted process is a wonderful way to work with colors and patterns. It's an adventure I think you'll enjoy.

Blue Stew by Mary Anne Caplinger, 1991, Wilkesboro, North Carolina. The title of this piece has a double meaning: Blue Stew refers not only to the blend of colors and designs, but also to my frustration with precision piecing.

INTRODUCTION

The method I use to create my woven quilts and wearable art may look a little unusual, but it's similar to traditional pieced or collaged techniques. And it's wonderfully simple: you tear or cut strips from two or more pieces of fabric and weave the strips to make a new "fabric." In fact, the process is easier than many other textile techniques because you assemble your new fabric on top of the batting and backing. When the weaving is finished, you're ready to start quilting. You'll be surprised and pleased at how quickly your fabric strips turn into a quilt top.

For those of you who are not weavers, I include "A Few Words About Weaving," a brief history of the development of weaving in the United States and an introduction to basic weaving terms. "Tools and Supplies" describes the equipment needed to get started. You'll be happy to know that no unusual weaving or sewing equipment is necessary. In this method, an ordinary tabletop replaces the traditional weaving loom. You probably have most of the necessary sewing supplies on hand.

Choosing fabrics is so much fun that many of us already have enough of a stash for a few—or more

than a few!—new quilts. In "Fabrics," you'll learn to see some of your favorite fabrics from a different perspective. The over-one, under-one weaving sequence hides parts of a print and highlights others, revealing color and pattern surprises as you work. I think you'll be fascinated with the sophisticated and unexpected effects.

"Let's Begin!" teaches you the basic woven and quilted process, with a small wall hanging, "Tropic Ice," as our work in progress. You can follow along and make this easy quilt or use the general instructions to create an original design.

One look at the "Woven and Quilted Projects" and you'll appreciate even more the versatility of this simple technique. The collection includes whimsical quilts, innovative wearable art, and one-of-a-kind decorating accessories. You'll find detailed instructions and helpful illustrations for all the projects in this section.

Whether you make quilts for your bed, your walls, or yourself, a woven piece will add to your quiltmaking skills and express your creativity and style. The book you hold in your hands will show you how.

Close-up of Peek-a-Boo Cats. See page 35 for full quilt.

A FEW WORDS ABOUT WEAVING

We are surrounded by fabric. Our clothing, furniture, and even cars rely on soft fabric to protect us from hard or cold surfaces. Yet the development of woven cloth is taken for granted to such an extent that history books rarely mention the first knotted and twined textiles. If we think about it though, the invention of the knot and the evolution of felting and weaving processes were just as revolutionary as the discovery of fire.

Once our ancestors learned to plait and twine rough grasses for baskets, they began to investigate the softer, thinner vegetable fibers. These could be pounded and then woven flat, first for mats and eventually for clothing. Whether for shelter or personal adornment, cloth making came before the development of pottery and metallurgy in all parts of the world. Major trade routes, such as the famous Silk Road, grew from the desire for beautiful, luxurious fabrics and the raw materials to produce them.

When the first colonists came to the New World, weaving looms and patterns were among their most important possessions. Although most colonies had small factories with professional weavers, the majority of households produced their own woven cloth. All of the yarn for the factory, as well as for the household, was homespun. The whole family was involved in the effort to grow, clean, and prepare flax for spinning and weaving linen cloth.

Throughout the early and middle years of the nineteenth century, along with the growth of factories and professional traveling weavers, hand weaving on household looms was common. Wool from Merino sheep and cotton from plantations in the South provided raw materials for additional yarns to be used with the familiar linen.

By the end of the nineteenth century, however, the average family was much less involved in the production of woven cloth. The invention of the spinning mule and the power loom completely changed the processes of commercial weaving and spinning. These machines, while much more efficient than hand spinning and hand weaving, were too large and too costly for home use. As the factory system grew, it rapidly incorporated the processes that were formerly done by household members.

Today, virtually all our fabric is produced in large factories, and the average person is far removed from the cloth-making process. But the fascination with cloth itself remains—unusual fibers, tantalizing colors, and new finishing techniques for commercial clothing and household textiles find a ready market. Hand weaving still attracts many people who want to experience the process and many more people who appreciate the product made by a human hand.

Ordinarily, weaving is done on a loom with thin yarns or threads interlaced to make the cloth. For the woven and quilted projects in this book, traditional yarns are replaced by strips of fabric 1" wide or wider. Instead of spinning cotton or wool to make the warp and weft, you'll tear long, narrow pieces of fabric and use them to weave on a much larger scale. With this technique, your weaving will develop quickly, but you'll still have the pleasure of working with your hands in the ancient way.

A 200-year-old weaving loom on display at Hickory Ridge Homestead Museum, Boone, N.C. (Courtesy of Hickory Ridge Homestead Museum; photo by Lee Bloom)

WEAVING TERMS

Two words used in this book may not be familiar to you—"warp" and "weft." If you look closely at a piece of cotton shirting or quilting fabric with a magnifying glass, you'll be able to distinguish two sets of threads that cross each other.

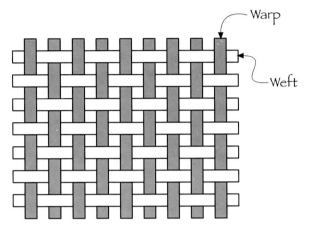

Warp. The lengthwise threads, parallel to the selvage edges of finished cloth, are called the warp. The warp threads are attached to the loom during weaving. Because these threads are strong and stable, most fabric pieces for clothing and quilts are cut with the warp running in a vertical direction, also known as the lengthwise grain.

When torn on the lengthwise grain, many fabrics stretch and tend to have long ravels. If you wish to use a fabric with a vertical design for a woven and quilted project, it's better to cut strips rather than tear them.

Weft. The horizontal threads that run from selvage to selvage are called the weft, also known as the cross grain. In the weaving process, the weft threads are interlaced with the warp threads to form cloth. If you hold a piece of fabric with one selvage in each hand and stretch it, you'll find that the weft threads are usually more elastic than the warp. Most of the projects in this book use fabric strips that are torn on the cross grain, that is, from selvage to selvage.

Bias. The bias is another term used when talking about fabric grain. Bias refers to any diagonal line that intersects the lengthwise and crosswise threads. When fabric is cut on the true bias (at a 45° angle to the selvage), it has maximum elasticity and doesn't ravel much. Some of the fabrics used in this book were cut on the bias to take advantage of a particular design. For example, stripes and other vertical designs gain energy and movement when cut on the bias.

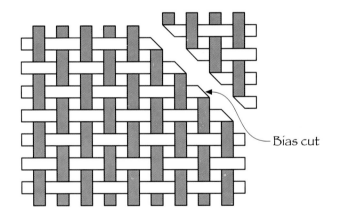

The proper work surface and a few tools and supplies will speed your weaving and help you create neat, straight woven and quilted pieces.

WORK SURFACES

In the traditional weaving process, warp threads are held on a loom under tension while the weft threads are woven under and over them. Even though you won't be threading your fabric strips on a loom, you'll need to hold them taut.

A collection of measuring, marking, cutting, and construction tools

Table. You can use any flat tabletop for weaving. In my workshops, two people usually share an eight-foot Formica®-top table. For proper tension, we secure the fabric to the tabletop with masking tape. If you need to work on a good kitchen or dining room table, cover it with cardboard or layers of newspaper to prevent accidental pin pricks. Lay an extra-long piece of muslin over the cardboard or newspapers; wrap the fabric to the underside of the table and tape it in place.

Collapsible cardboard cutting table. This table, 32" x 55", is my favorite surface for working on woven projects because I can stick pins directly into the tabletop. It's easy to adjust the tension or change strips during weaving. The table is lightweight and has removable legs, allowing you to store a work in progress. You can order the table with legs that are 34" or 40" long; choose the height that's most convenient for you. See Resources on page 79.

Work space board. An alternative to using a separate table is a work space board. This surface is a large heat- and water-resistant board covered with cotton fabric printed in a 1" grid. The board folds in half for easy storage of a work in progress. The large size, 51" x 33", covers an average dining room table. The junior size, 21" x 27", packs conveniently for a class. See Resources on page 79.

Quilt frame. You can also use a traditional floor quilt frame for weaving. Install the backing and batting as usual, then pin the warp strips to the batting at the top of the frame. You'll need to experiment to determine how to pin the other ends of the warp strips for the necessary tension. You may need to complete the top half of your project, roll it on the frame, and continue working on the lower half.

Pressing surface. A portable pressing pad, 13" x 14", is just the right size for small weaving projects. One side of this reversible square is a rotary-cutting mat; the other side is a cushion marked with a 1" grid. See Resources on page 79.

MEASURING, MARKING, AND CUTTING TOOLS

You may tear or cut your warp and weft strips. If you choose to tear your strips, you'll need a tape measure and scissors to measure and mark the fabric.

If you choose to cut your strips, you'll need a rotary cutter, mat, and ruler. Because strips for weaving must be perfectly straight, I prefer to cut a single layer of fabric rather than folding the fabric, as you would for other rotary cutting.

Rotary cutter. A rotary cutter looks like a pizza cutter with a protective shield for the blade. Rotary cutters are available in three sizes. Many quilters prefer the two larger sizes because they feel it's easier to cut through several layers with a large blade.

Rotary cutters have extremely sharp blades. Never leave the blade exposed, even for a moment. Rotary cutters with manually engaged safety shields are the safest. Get in the habit of engaging the safety shield as soon as you finish each cut. Automatically retracting safety shields are not as safe because the shield may retract when dropped or touched.

Rotary mat. A self-healing rotary mat holds the fabric in place and protects both the blade and the work surface. Mats come in several sizes; choose the most convenient size for your work surface. The 32" x 55" mat fits the top of the collapsible cardboard cutting table. Although it's expensive, this large mat is a good investment.

Rotary rulers. These rulers come in different sizes and grid formats. Compare the marks and colors on various rulers to see which you prefer. For woven and quilted projects, it's helpful to have a ruler that is at least 5" wide and 24" long.

Markers. Chalk is best for marking warp and weft guidelines.

Other tools. To check the alignment of the strips as you weave, use two yardsticks placed at right angles. A large acrylic square, 12" x 12", or a T-square will also work.

CONSTRUCTION TOOLS

Weaving needles. Weaving by hand is easy and fun. You may, however, prefer a flat weaving needle or a long craft needle with a large eye, such as the kind used in dollmaking.

You can also make a satisfactory needle from a plastic milk carton. Cut a strip approximately 1" x 5"; taper one end and cut a 1" slit close to the other end for the eye. Lightly sand the edges.

Pins. Very fine glass-head silk pins are the easiest to slide through the layers of fabric.

Fusible web. Paper-backed fusible web allows you to change strips in the middle of a row. Follow the manufacturer's instructions carefully.

Iron. A good steam iron makes pressing the fabric strips fast and easy. You'll also need your iron for fusing strips.

Sewing machine. Have your machine in good working order before you begin: remove any lint, oil if necessary, and adjust the tension.

Thread. For quilting, assorted colors and types of thread add visual excitement to your woven surface. Experiment with rayon, silk, and metallic threads.

Needles. For machine quilting, a medium-size (85/11) universal point needle will usually go through the layers of fabric and batting easily. Also consider the thread when you're choosing a needle for machine quilting.

If your machine begins to skip stitches, try a needle made especially for quilting; it has a very sharp point and a large eye. You can also use a stretch needle, which is longer than a regular needle and has an anti-static coating. Another option is a "jeans" needle, which has a very fine, sharp point. Both stretch and jeans needles come in a variety of sizes.

For hand quilting, you may wish to experiment with a larger-size needle than you normally use because you'll be quilting through an extra layer of fabric. If you still have difficulty quilting, try using a needle lubricant.

Masking tape. Use masking tape to anchor the backing and batting to your work surface before you begin weaving.

In the woven and quilted process, you assemble the layers, known as the quilt sandwich, as you would for a traditional quilt top, batting, and backing. The difference is that the order is reversed: instead of constructing a quilt top and then selecting batting and backing, you lay out the batting and backing and weave your strips on top of them. Since the assembly process for woven quilts begins with the backing, I'll discuss it first.

BACKING

Choose a lightweight, sturdy fabric for the reverse side of the quilt. Many quilters use unbleached muslin for the backing on all of their quilts, but you can have fun selecting a backing that coordinates with your woven quilt top.

If the finished size of the quilt is less than the width of your backing fabric, you won't need to piece the backing; simply cut it to the correct length.

If the finished size is wider than your backing fabric, you'll need to piece the backing. Generally, the backing consists of three pieces: one width of fabric in the center and a partial width seamed on either side. You may choose to piece the backing using several related fabrics.

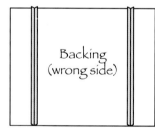

Backing
(wrong side)

BATTING

Batting is the puffy layer between the woven top and the backing. When the three layers of a quilt sandwich (top, batting, and backing) are quilted, the areas between the stitching stand out in relief.

Many kinds of batting are available to quilters today. Most battings are made of cotton or polyester, or a blend of the two. The choice of fiber content is purely personal.

Batting thickness varies from ⅛" to almost 2". Because the woven quilt top has two layers of fabric, it's important to minimize the bulk and weight. Choose a thin, smooth, very lightweight batting. I prefer Thermore® by Hobbs. Even low-loft batting is too puffy for the woven and quilted projects in this book. If low-loft batting is the only lightweight batting available to you, split it into two layers and use only one.

Prewashed cotton flannel is another option. Sometimes the batting is eliminated altogether, especially for clothing.

Most cotton or polyester batting doesn't need to be prewashed before it's used. Check the package for directions.

THE WOVEN TOP

In the woven and quilted process, narrow strips of fabric replace traditional weaving yarns used for the warp and weft. You can tear or cut these fabric strips. Right away, three questions come to mind: Which fabrics are suitable? What will the design of the fabric look like when it's torn or cut into strips? How will the edges of the strips be finished?

Suitable Fabrics

You have few limitations when it comes to fabrics for woven and quilted projects. Fabrics that don't tear easily can be cut on the cross grain. Those that ravel can be cut on the bias, or the edges finished in one of several ways. The weight of the fabric is the most important consideration, especially if you plan to hand quilt, because a woven top has two layers of fabric. For this reason, lightweight fabrics are generally easiest to work with.

Cotton or cotton blends are good choices for your first project because they possess a slight nap that helps hold the strips in place until they're sewn.

Once you've woven several projects using traditional quilting cottons, try working with knit, lamé, silk, and wool. This is a wonderful opportunity to try unusual fabrics that may not be appropriate for other types of quilting.

Fabrics suitable for weaving include (from the top) cotton, interlock knit, lamé, wool, linen, and China silk.

Fabric Preparation

You can wash your woven and quilted projects, just as you would traditional quilts and wearables. If you tear your fabric strips and remove the ravels, the edges will remain stable, although they will soften slightly with washing. If you cut the strips, some raveling will occur with washing, but it's not usually a problem. To see how the strips will look after washing, make a small, 12" x 12" woven and quilted sample and wash it. Of course, you can dry-clean your projects if washing seems risky.

If you're planning to wash your woven and quilted pieces, prepare cottons and other washable fabrics by prewashing to remove the sizing. Wash the fabric in the washing machine or soak it in a basin of warm water. When prewashing dark fabrics, check the rinse water for traces of dye. Continue to rinse until the water is clear. If the fabric keeps running after several washings, it's best to eliminate it from your collection.

If you intend to dry-clean the finished project, lay a damp press cloth on top of the fabric and lightly press with an iron.

Print Styles

All prints are appropriate for woven and quilted work. To create vitality and visual interest in a woven piece, choose fabrics that are related, perhaps by common colors, yet varied, perhaps in the scale of the design. This harmonious look usually calls for a mix of print styles.

Many of the fabrics today feature flowers or other motifs taken from nature. These prints are often described as naturalistic.

Prints inspired by nature include bright, splashy florals, bountiful fruits, and woodsy motifs.

Naturalistic prints are so beautiful and appealing that we tend to overlook plaids, geometrics, and abstract designs. These fabrics lend energy and movement to woven and quilted pieces.

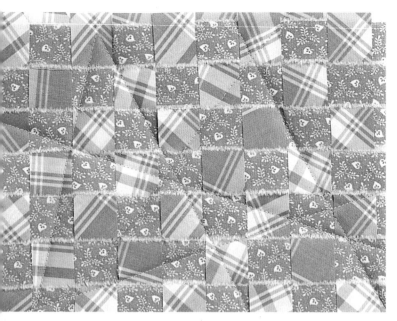

Strips of a large plaid, cut off-grain, and a small geometric print create a jumble of lines and pattern in this blue-and-white example.

Whimsical faces, Halloween motifs, dreamy landscapes, cowboy boots, and—of all things!—alligators on roller skates are real conversation starters.

Conversation prints make up another category of print styles. These include off-beat, comic, and bizarre combinations of incongruous figures and elements.

One of these unusual fabrics can easily inspire a quilt design. After seeing fabric printed in a design of neon shoes, I started thinking about my two sis-

ters' fondness for shoes and what I could do with that idea. As a result, I've started collecting fabric with shoe motifs and buttons in the shape of shoes. I'm not sure where the idea will lead me, but I'm getting ready with a stash of fabrics!

Most of the projects in this book are done with printed fabrics, but solids are very effective in woven and quilted pieces. Look at groups of solid fabrics in rainbow colors or the packets of hand-dyed gradated solids you see at quilt shows. Classic checkerboard designs (one dark and one light solid) or gingham looks (one dark, one medium, and one light solid) are easy to achieve by weaving.

Shopping for Fabrics

When you're searching for fabrics, keep an open mind—you never know when you'll see the inspiration for your next, and best, quilt. Browse in several fabric stores or quilt shops if you have that luxury. Study the colors and shapes in fabrics because these are the important design features in a woven top.

Most florals, plaids, and conversation prints have a wide range of colors. Look carefully at all the colors in the fabric—the lights, the darks, and especially the neutral or bridge colors. The neutral greens, browns, and grays are easy to overlook in favor of brighter colors, but they play an important role. Neutrals provide visual relief and depth, and these qualities create rhythm in a quilt.

A Theme Fabric

Generally, I start with one large-scale print to establish a color scheme. The design of this "theme" fabric should cover most of the space; too much plain background can make the finished weaving appear dull. A multicolored fabric gives me the most options when I choose coordinating fabrics. I often look in the drapery department of a fabric store to find a print with large flowers or bold brush strokes. While I'm looking at the design, I try to determine if the fabric will tear or cut easily.

Many home-decorating fabrics are too heavy to hand quilt, but nearly all can be machine quilted. In general, if the fabric tears easily, it can be quilted by hand or machine.

Coordinating Fabrics

I usually select coordinating fabrics that are in the same color family as the theme fabric but are smaller in scale and varied in style. When you choose coordinating fabrics, plan to spend time looking at many possibilities. This process of considering fabrics has been referred to as "auditioning." It's the most effective way, short of tearing strips and weaving, to see how fabrics look together.

In the fabric store or at home, stack your fabrics one on top of the other so that an inch of each fabric shows. Then stand back to see if you have a variety of light and dark, bright and subtle, small- and large-scale fabrics in your selection. If it's not immediately obvious, squint while looking at your stack. Squinting removes the distraction of individual shapes and allows you to concentrate on the color and value relationships. If you don't see enough excitement and contrast in the fabrics you've chosen, substitute others until you're satisfied with the mix. Set your coordinating fabrics aside and turn your attention back to your theme fabric.

Putting Together a Color Scheme

To create a successful color scheme using your theme fabric and coordinating fabrics, you must first ask, What will the design of the theme fabric look like when it's torn into strips? You'll be amazed at how different a fabric looks when it's torn or cut.

To get an idea of the effect, cut a few 1"-wide strips of paper or gather several yardsticks. Lay your theme fabric flat on a table or the floor. Lay the paper strips or yardsticks on the fabric, leaving about 1" of fabric between them. Now look at what's happened to the fabric design. You'll probably find it difficult to distinguish the motifs; instead, you'll see curved or angled lines and small areas of color.

With the strips of paper or yardsticks still on your fabric, examine the colors to see which ones pop out. This gives you a clue as to which of your coordinating fabrics will be most effective with the theme fabric. The photos on the following page show some of the possibilities using a large-scale theme print and smaller-scale coordinating fabrics.

Covering a large-scale print with strips of paper gives you a preview of how the fabric will look when torn into strips and woven.

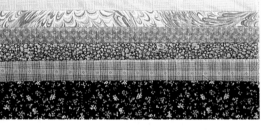

Some fabrics that seem ideal may not "work" with your theme print. In this example, the dark strips recede into the background, while the tangerine strips overpower the print. The white provides good contrast without dominating the theme print.

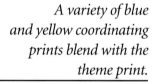

A variety of blue and yellow coordinating prints blend with the theme print.

Soft red and green weft strips harmonize beautifully with the theme print. Because the coordinating fabrics repeat colors in the theme print, your eye still "reads" some of the large motifs.

Some fabrics have small, evenly spaced repeat designs, which are fun to weave. With careful planning, you can isolate a line of motifs and frame individual elements, such as the teacups shown here. To isolate motifs, the warp and weft strips should be slightly narrower than the space between motifs to allow "breathing room" for each motif.

Selecting an Edge Finish

In traditional piecing and appliqué, the raw edges are hidden by the seams or turned under. Seaming or turning the edges makes a quilt top sturdy and gives a neat, flat appearance.

In the woven and quilted process, the strips are not sewn together, which means that the raw edges are exposed. You have two choices: to leave the edges of the strips unfinished or to finish them. The decision depends on the types of fabrics you're using, the look you prefer, and how much time you want to spend getting that look.

Either option, unfinished or finished edges, has advantages, so experiment with your fabrics before beginning a project.

Unfinished Edges

Fabric strips may be torn or cut and the edges left unfinished.

Tearing your fabric into strips is fast, easy—and a great stress reliever! Most cottons, cotton blends, and medium-weight silks tear easily across the grain. You'll need to remove the long ravels after you tear your strips, but once you press the strips, the edges should not continue to ravel.

Torn edges on cotton fabrics add a casual touch and keep your quilt from being too serious. I find that unfinished edges are a great conversation starter, especially with silk or silklike fabrics. Although we've seen more washed and sueded silk in recent years, there is still a mystique surrounding this luxurious fabric. I love the surprising combination of casual torn edges on an elegant fabric—not ragged or scruffy edges, just an unexpected soft fringe.

Some prints, especially those with black or dark backgrounds, may reveal small dots of white at the edges when they're torn. These specks occur because tearing pulls the warp threads just enough to move

The width of the warp and weft strips is determined by the size of the teacups.

Unfinished edges (from the left): two torn strips, two cut strips, and a roll of precut cotton strips.

them out of alignment. With some fabrics, tearing noticeably changes the color at the edges; with other fabrics, it doesn't. This possibility is another reason to tear a few test strips before beginning a project.

Cutting the strips with scissors or a rotary cutter and mat (see page 9) is necessary for specialty fabrics such as lamé, tricot, or knits. Striped fabrics or those with small designs arranged in vertical or horizontal rows also need to be cut rather than torn because they are rarely printed with the design on the straight of grain.

Strips that are cut will ravel because you inevitably cut across threads. Don't remove the ravels—if you do, the edges of the strips will look uneven. The raveling is not usually objectionable, but if occasional ravels don't fit your design concept, try one of the finishing methods described below.

Cutting some or all of the strips gives you a great deal of flexibility in how you use a printed fabric. To add a strong directional element to your woven piece, try cutting strips with curved edges. Another way to bring movement to a design is to cut striped fabric on the diagonal. Just remember that the bias edges will stretch easily and must be handled with care.

Strips of fabric on rolls are an alternative to cutting or tearing the strips yourself. Weavers often use fabric strips as weft when they're making rugs. Check with a shop that sells yarn or weaving supplies to see if they have rolls of fabric strips, similar to rolls of ribbon. One example of this "yarn" is Poppanna from Finland. It's actually a ⅜"-wide bias strip of cotton fabric that comes in about forty wonderful colors. See the photo on page 42 and Resources on page 79.

Finished Edges

If you decide to finish the edges of your strips, you have two options: overcasting or folding under the raw edges. Overcasting the cut edges or serging the strips using decorative thread can add beautiful accents to your woven surface. For highlights, consider using metallic or rayon thread in a shade darker or lighter than the fabric. You may want to try different colors of thread on adjacent strips or perhaps a variegated thread.

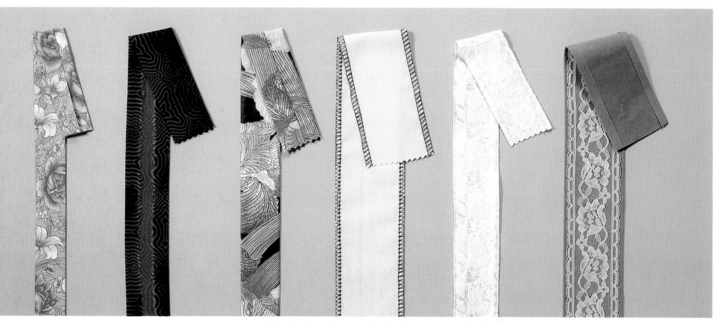

Finished edges (from the left): edges folded to overlap on the back, edges folded so a hint of the wrong side shows, a fabric tube, serged edges, ribbon, and lace.

Folding under the cut edges gives your woven piece a quiet, elegant look. Cut each strip twice the finished width plus ¼"and fold the cut edges lengthwise to overlap ¼" at the center back. Press the strip flat, turn it over, and weave with the smooth side up. For an example of weaving using folded strips, see "Circles of Violet" on page 57.

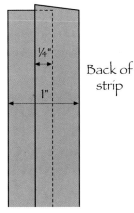

To create a different look, cut and fold the strips so that a hint of the wrong side shows. This variation is very effective with a fabric whose wrong side is just as appealing as its right side, or a fabric whose wrong side contrasts sharply with its right side. For 1" finished strips, cut the strips 1¾", then fold each edge ⅜" to reveal ¼" of the wrong side.

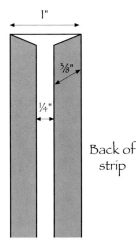

Since you're adding, in effect, another layer to the quilt top when you fold the edges of the strips, consider the weight of the fabric before you choose this method.

Fabric tubes are another variation on folded-edge strips. Cut each strip twice the desired finished width plus ½". With right sides together, stitch lengthwise, using a ¼"-wide seam allowance. With the tip of your iron, press the seam open. Turn the tube right side out and press it with the seam centered on the back.

Another option is to stitch a tube and leave it unturned. You can start with the right or the wrong sides together, depending on the colors in the fabric. Press the seam open.

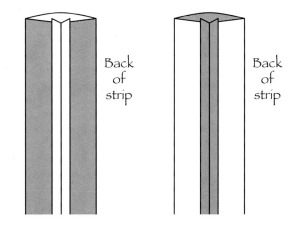

Because a fabric tube adds an additional layer to the quilt top, it's probably only suitable for very lightweight fabrics.

Decorative ribbons, with their finished edges, are easy to use. However, ribbons are sometimes woven very tightly, and it is difficult to hand quilt through them. They're also more expensive than fabric. But you'll find many beautiful ribbons in fabric stores, and they make a nice accent when mixed with fabric strips.

Lace adds a delicate touch to woven and quilted projects. If the lace is fairly heavy and densely woven, you can weave it as you would a fabric strip. If it's narrow, lightweight, or has uneven edges, lay the lace on top of a fabric strip; anchor with a dot of fabric glue every inch or so. Treat this double strip as one when you weave. For an example of weaving with ribbon and lace, see "Lavender 'n Lace" on page 61.

LET'S BEGIN!

This section introduces you to the basic woven and quilted process, using a small wall hanging as an example. "Tropic Ice" is an ideal warm-up project: it's easy to make, yet it includes all the elements of a woven and quilted piece. Read the instructions from start to finish, then gather your fabrics and supplies and follow along as you weave your own version of this simple project. Once you've finished, you'll find it easy to apply these basic instructions to other projects in the book or to your own designs.

Tropic Ice by Mary Anne Caplinger, 1994, Wilkesboro, North Carolina, 17" x 23".

THE WOVEN AND QUILTED PROCESS

Parts of the process described in this section resemble traditional quiltmaking, but some steps will be new to you. Never fear! Weaving with fabric is easy, and you'll be amazed at how quickly your strips turn into a quilt top.

The step-by-step instructions that follow are for "Tropic Ice," but you can use them to make other woven and quilted pieces. If you're working on a project or acquainting yourself with the basic process, it's still helpful to read all the instructions—the "Tropic Ice" examples will help you visualize the steps.

Getting Started

Begin a woven and quilted project by determining its size and selecting the materials.

1. Estimate the finished size of the piece. Think in general terms—small (up to 24" on a side), medium (up to 54" on a side), or large (more than 54" on a side).

   "Tropic Ice" is a small, rectangular wall hanging or table mat that measures 17" x 23". This is the finished size.

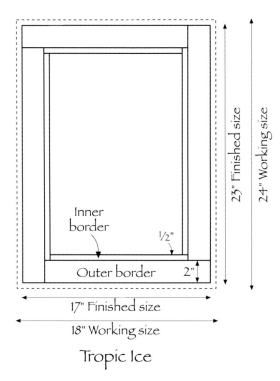

Tropic Ice

2. Choose your theme and coordinating fabrics; for guidelines, see "The Woven Top" on page 10. "Tropic Ice" features a bright tropical print as the theme fabric. The royal blue background is a good contrast to the lively flowers and fruit. Strong colors in the print suggest several coordinating fabrics.

Crisp green and white fabrics cool down hot tropical colors in the theme print. A small-scale jelly bean print repeats the bright hues.

3. Choose the backing and batting; for guidelines, see "Backing" and "Batting" on page 10. Using the finished-size measurements from step 1, cut the backing and batting, allowing an extra inch in length and width for trimming the piece after quilting. For "Tropic Ice," the backing is 18" wide and 24" long. This is the working size.

4. Layer the batting and backing. Cut the batting ¼" smaller on all edges to allow the backing to extend slightly beyond the batting. Lay the backing right side down on your work surface and center the batting on the backing. Secure the batting and the backing with pins or masking tape across the upper and lower edges.

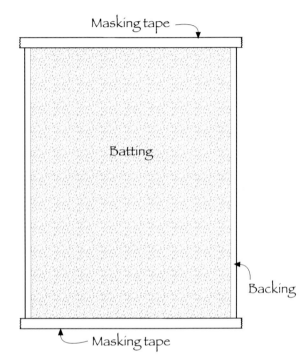

Masking tape

Batting

Backing

Masking tape

5. Determine the width of the outer border. If you're making one of the projects in the book, the outer border widths are determined for you. The outer border on "Tropic Ice" is 2". If you're designing your own project, it's best to choose a whole number for the finished width of the outer border, including the portion that is encased by the binding.

Because the borders cover portions of the weaving, the woven area that shows is smaller than the finished piece. You may wonder if you can get away with weaving just the area framed by the borders. You can't; for stability during quilting, the weaving must extend all the way to the edges.

Preparing the Strips

If you look carefully at the warp in the finished version of "Tropic Ice," you'll notice that the continuity of the fabric's design is maintained. That is,

your eye can still "read" parts of the design as it appeared before the fabric was torn into strips. You achieve this visual continuity by tearing or cutting the warp strips from a rectangle of fabric and arranging the strips in order.

If you're using solid fabrics or prints that don't require keeping the strips in order, you can tear or cut your strips all the way across the width of the fabric, then cut them to the lengths needed. In most of the projects beginning on page 35, the strips are prepared in this way. Turn to "Preparing Strips from a Full Width of Fabric" on page 23 for step-by-step instructions.

For woven and quilted projects that maintain the design continuity of the fabric, such as "Tropic Ice," follow these steps to prepare the warp strips:

1. Determine the width and length of the warp strips. In woven and quilted projects, strips are usually from ¾" to 1½" wide. It's possible to tear a ½"- or even ¼"-wide strip, but only with fabrics that are very closely woven. The strips for "Tropic Ice" are 1" wide. The strips are equal in length to the working length. The strips for "Tropic Ice" are 24" long.

2. Determine the number of filler strips. You won't use "good" fabric strips for the areas covered by the outer border; instead, you'll use filler strips torn or cut from muslin or scrap fabric. (See the photos on page 22 for examples of filler strips.) Filler strips are usually 1" wide. You will need enough filler strips under each border to equal the finished width of the outer border. "Tropic Ice" requires two 1"-wide filler strips under each outer border because the finished width of the outer border is 2".

3. Determine the dimensions of the warp-strip rectangle. This rectangle is equal in length to the working length. The warp-strip rectangle for "Tropic Ice" is 24" long.

To determine the width of the warp-strip rectangle, subtract the inches required for the filler strips from the finished width of the project. The warp-strip rectangle for "Tropic Ice" is 14" wide (18" − 4" for four 1"-wide filler strips).

4. Prepare the warp strips. To create a straight edge, tear or cut on the cross grain close to the cut end of the fabric. From this torn or cut edge, measure the width of your warp-strip rectangle (14" for "Tropic Ice") along one selvage and mark with a snip; tear or cut for a distance equal to the length of the warp-strip rectangle (24" for "Tropic Ice"). Tear or cut the side opposite the selvage to complete the rectangle.

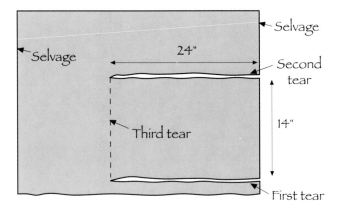

The rectangle is the approximate amount of warp fabric needed. When you pull off the ravels to neaten the strips after they're torn, they may shrink a little in width, and you may need another strip to finish your weaving. If so, tear an extra strip and add it to the left edge.

5. Place a piece of masking tape on the fabric rectangle along the selvage to keep from tearing or cutting the strips all the way. Mark the fabric lightly along the opposite edge in increments equal to the strip width (1" for "Tropic Ice").

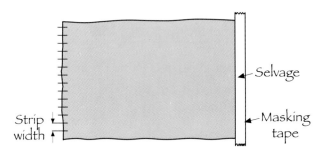

6. Snip the fabric at the marks and tear each strip across the width to within ½" of the selvage. The edges will curl and be full of ravels. At this point, your fabric will look like a "grass skirt." Attach it to the wall or lay it on a table with the tape at the top.

Your "grass skirt" looks like anything but a work of art!

If you choose to cut the strips with a rotary cutter rather than tear them, press the fabric so that it lies flat under the ruler. Following the guidelines on the ruler, cut the strips to within ½" of one selvage.

7. Prepare the warp filler strips. Tear or cut and press the number of filler strips required. For "Tropic Ice," tear 4 strips, each 1" x 24". If you're making one of the projects in the book, check the yardage chart to determine the number and width of the warp filler strips.

8. Position the warp strips. Lay the appropriate number of filler strips (2 for "Tropic Ice") on top of the batting at the right edge. Beginning at the right edge of the torn rectangle—your grass skirt—snip the remaining selvage edge of the first strip. Pull off the ravels and masking tape and press the strip. Lay the strip on top of the batting at the right, next to the inner filler strip.

Two warp filler strips and the first warp print strip

9. Continue laying strips until all the warp strips have been placed on top of the batting in order. End with the remaining filler strips. Check to make sure that all the warp strips are snug against each other but not overlapping. If the warp strips are perfectly aligned, you'll see the fabric pattern almost as it looked before you tore or cut the strips.

10. Anchor the strips. To keep the warp straight and provide the right amount of tension, use straight pins or masking tape to secure the strips at the upper and lower edges.

Anchor the warp strips with masking tape.

11. Prepare the weft strips. Gather the fabrics for the weft strips. Figure the dimensions of the weft strips as follows:

The weft strips can be as wide as the warp strips, or the weft strips can vary in width. The weft strips for "Tropic Ice" are the same width as the warp strips: 1".

The length of the weft strips is the same as the working width. The weft strips for "Tropic Ice" are 18" long.

As you did for the warp strips, tear or cut on the cross grain close to the cut end of the fabric to create a straight edge. Measure and snip the strips at one selvage, then tear or cut the strips all the way to the other selvage.

Cut the strips to the lengths specified in the project. For "Tropic Ice," you'll need the following number of 18" weft strips: 4 filler muslin, 12 white-on-white, 4 green gingham, and 3 jelly bean.

PREPARING STRIPS FROM A FULL WIDTH OF FABRIC

For woven and quilted projects that do not require keeping the warp strips in order, you can tear or cut both the warp and weft strips across the full width of the fabric. To tear your strips, follow these steps:

1. Determine the warp and weft strip width and length. In woven and quilted projects, strips are usually from ¾" to 1½" wide. It's possible to tear a ½"- or even ¼"-strip, but only with fabrics that are very closely woven. The strips are equal in length to the working length of the project.

2. Create a straight edge. Tear crosswise close to the cut end of the fabric to create a straight edge.

3. Mark the strips. Measure and mark the fabric lightly along one selvage in increments equal to the strip width. Mark as many warp and weft strips as you need.

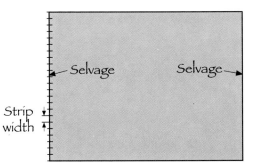

4. Tear the strips. Snip the fabric at the marks and tear each strip all the way across the width; snip the opposite selvage. The edges will curl and be full of ravels. Remove the ravels and press the strips.

5. Determine the number of warp filler strips needed; see step 2 on page 20.

6. Prepare the warp filler strips; see step 7, page 22.

7. Position the warp strips. Lay the appropriate number of filler strips on top of the batting at the right edge. Lay the first print strip on top of the batting, next to the inner filler strip.

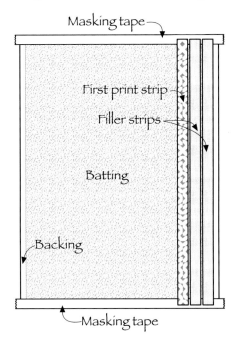

8. Continue laying strips until all the warp strips have been placed on top of the batting. End with the remaining filler strips. Check to make sure that all the warp strips are snug against each other but not overlapping.

9. Anchor the strips. To keep the warp straight and provide the right amount of tension, use straight pins or masking tape to secure the strips at the upper and lower edges.

10. See "Weaving the Weft Strips" on the following page to begin weaving.

Weaving the Weft Strips

Finally, after all the preparations, you're ready to weave.

1. Starting at the top, pick up a filler weft strip and slide it under every other warp strip with your fingers. You will quickly develop the "over one, under one" rhythm. When you reach the opposite edge, hold the ends in your fingers and pull the strip taut to make it lie straight and flat.

   Lay your rotary ruler on top of the strip and adjust any areas that aren't straight. Pin each end of the strip to the batting and backing.

A weaving needle guides the weft strip over and under the warp.

The first filler weft strip

If you're not comfortable weaving with your fingers, use a weaving or craft needle. You can also make your own needle; see "Weaving needles" on page 9.

Two weft filler strips and the first print weft strip

2. Continue weaving. Smooth and straighten the warp strips. Weave the second filler strip, reversing the over one, under one pattern. The second filler strip lies on top of each warp strip that the first filler strip went under. This sequence is much easier to do than it is to describe! The third weft strip, which is the first print strip, goes under the same warp strips as the first filler strip.

Weave the remaining weft strips, referring to the weaving diagram shown below for the strip placement. After every other strip, use your rotary ruler or yardsticks to make sure that the warp and weft are straight. Finish weaving with the two remaining filler strips.

A WEAVING DIAGRAM FOR "TROPIC ICE"

The diagram at the right shows at a glance the weaving sequence for "Tropic Ice." In this illustration, the warp and weft strips are spaced for clarity. Each fabric is represented by a different pattern; the filler strips at the edges are plain.

The weaving sequence for each project in the book will be illustrated in the same way. The fabrics will be indicated by different patterns, and the filler strips will always be plain.

◨ Tropical print

☐ White-on-white

▥ Green gingham

⊡ Jelly bean print

Tropic Ice

The chart below lists the materials needed for "Tropic Ice." The total yardage for each fabric is given first, then it's broken down into the number of pieces and their sizes.

NOTE

In some instances, quarter yards are generous for the number of strips you'll tear or cut. Extra inches have been allowed because your fabric may not be cut on the straight grain when you buy it. If that's the case, you'll lose a little fabric when you tear or cut the edge before you prepare the strips. If you're using scraps, you may be able to get away with less than the yardage given in the list.

MATERIALS
44"-wide fabrics

¾ yd. yellow solid for backing, inner border, and sleeve

1 yd. tropical print for warp, outer border, and binding

¼ yd. white-on-white print for weft

¼ yd. green gingham for weft

¼ yd. jelly bean print for weft

¼ yd. muslin for filler strips

½ yd. very lightweight batting*

*Be sure to read "Batting" on page 10; low-loft battings are too thick for woven and quilted projects.

Fabric	Used for	Number of Pieces	Size
Yellow solid	Backing	1	18" x 24"
	Inner border	2	2" x 21"
	Inner border	2	2" x 15"
	Sleeve	1	10" x 17"
Tropical print	Warp	14	1" x 24"
	Outer border	2	2½" x 23"
	Outer border	2	2½" x 17"
	Binding	1	2½" x 95"
White-on-white	Weft	12	1" x 18"
Green gingham	Weft	4	1" x 18"
Jelly bean print	Weft	3	1" x 18"
Muslin	Warp	2	1" x 24"
	Weft	2	1" x 18"
Batting		1	18" x 24"

Changing Fabrics in the Middle of a Row

Sometimes, it's effective to see only a small area of color in a row of weaving, rather than an entire warp or weft strip of the fabric. As you weave, you can easily attach a strip of one fabric to another and hide the join under a cross strip. The change can be made in a warp or weft row.

Changing fabrics in the middle of the row gives you much more flexibility in design; instead of "seeing what you get" when you weave the strips, you can deliberately alter the pattern or color of your design.

To join a strip of fabric B to a strip of fabric A, cut the ends of the strips so that they will overlap under the nearest cross strip. Apply a ½" square of paper-backed fusible web to the end of strip A on the right side. Peel off the paper and place strip B on top of strip A. Fuse the ends, following the manufacturer's instructions.

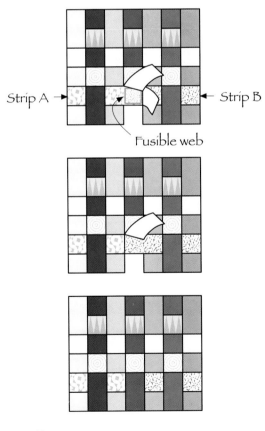

Pin Basting

Once the weaving is completed, you're ready to prepare your piece for quilting. Take the time to do a good job of pin basting. Layers that are well pinned are much easier to quilt. Careful pin basting helps prevent distortion of your woven piece during stitching and eliminates unwanted tucks or puckers.

1. Choose a quilting design and, if necessary, mark it. If you quilt by machine, you can center the presser foot on each strip. If you quilt by hand, you'll probably want to mark the quilting lines.

2. Check the alignment of the warp and weft. Straighten the strips one last time if necessary.

3. Pin-baste every other intersection of warp and weft strips. Place the pins so that you can easily remove them as you stitch. For hand quilting, follow the same procedure using safety pins.

Machine Quilting

With your machine in good working order and your woven piece well basted, you're ready to machine quilt. The machine quilting in "Tropic Ice" consists of straight stitching using a regular presser foot. It couldn't be simpler!

Begin quilting at the right edge. Starting at the edge is different from most machine quilting, which begins in the middle of a piece. However, machine quilting is usually done on a pieced or appliquéd top that is well secured by the time it's put under the machine. Because the strips in a woven and quilted piece are held in place only with pins, it's best to begin at the edge.

1. Quilt the warp rows. Quilt the first warp row, stitching in the center of the strip and removing the pins as you come to them. Quilt the remaining warp rows. As you work toward the middle, roll the stitched portion into a tube.

2. Quilt the weft rows. Turn the woven top and quilt the weft rows in the same way.

   If you prefer not to machine quilt, there are many other options for holding the layers together. Try tying with yarn or floss or sewing buttons at each warp and weft strip intersection.

3. Straighten the edges. With the woven and quilted top flat on a table, measure the length through the center, from edge to edge; mark the

midpoint. Mark half the finished length (11½" for "Tropic Ice," whose finished length is 23") above and below the midpoint. Measure the length at the right edge; mark the midpoint and the same distance (11½" for "Tropic Ice") above and below the midpoint as you did at the center. Repeat on the left edge. Draw a horizontal line through the marks at the upper and lower edges and trim on the lines. (See diagram at right.)

Rotate the woven and quilted piece and straighten the other two sides, using the finished width measurement.

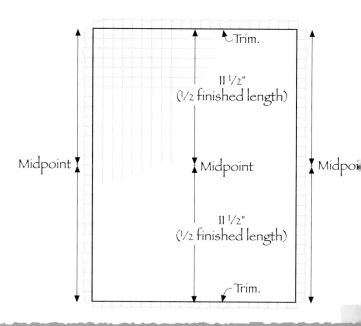

MACHINE-QUILTING HINTS

Machine quilting is ideal for woven quilt tops because it's easy to stitch through all the layers of fabric. If you've hesitated to machine quilt in the past, a woven piece is an ideal first project.

Following are machine-quilting tips that will make your work faster and more enjoyable.

✓ Have your machine clean and well oiled. If it's been a while since your machine was professionally cleaned and tuned, this is the time to do it. Lint in the gears or misadjusted tension disks will take away the fun of working on your quilt.

✓ Loosen the tension slightly. If your machine has a dial for the pressure setting, loosen it also. Often, the darning setting is best for machine quilting.

✓ Use a walking foot. This special presser foot is designed to guide all the layers in a quilt sandwich under the needle at the same time. If you're not familiar with a walking foot, ask your sewing-machine dealer for a demonstration. You'll be amazed at how evenly you can stitch with the proper presser foot.

✓ If it's the middle of the night and you can't wait to get started, try this trick: Sew for a few inches, then stop. Raise the presser foot and smooth the fabric. Lower the presser foot and sew for a few more inches, then stop. Raise the presser foot and repeat the process, smoothing the fabric and sewing a few inches at a time. Stopping and raising the presser foot releases some of the pressure on the top layer. This technique helps to keep the top, batting, and backing going under the needle at the same time.

✓ Use the proper needle. See "Needles" on page 9 for help in choosing the right machine-quilting needle. Because it's difficult to see the small nicks in a needle that can cause the thread to fray, you should change the needle at the beginning of each project.

✓ Use good-quality thread. Inexpensive thread breaks more easily, especially when going through several layers. The frustration is not worth the difference in price.

✓ Run the machine at a consistent speed. Find a comfortable speed that feeds the fabric under the needle evenly.

✓ For detailed machine-quilting instructions, refer to the books listed in Resources on page 79.

Adding the Borders

"Tropic Ice" and other projects in this book have two borders—a narrow inner border and a wider outer border. Instead of sewing two separate borders to the quilt top, you'll stitch both at the same time.

A narrow inner border and wider outer border frame Tropic Ice.

The narrow inner border consists of a folded piece that's not sewn on both long edges. Instead, the inner border is sandwiched between the woven quilt top and the outer border so that the fold overlaps the woven area slightly. At the corners, the border pieces overlap each other. A folded inner border is a great way to add an accent color to a woven top.

Choose a solid or miniprint fabric in a color found in small amounts in the theme fabric. The inner border on "Tropic Ice" is a bright yellow solid.

1. Determine the cut dimensions of the inner border pieces. You'll need four pieces, two for the upper and lower borders and two for the side borders. The cut width of the inner border pieces

is 2". When folded in half lengthwise and stitched using a ½"-wide seam, the finished width of the border will be ½".

The cut length of each inner border piece is equal to the distance between the inner filler strips plus 1". On "Tropic Ice," the distance between the inner warp filler strips is 14"; therefore, the cut length of the upper and lower border pieces is 15" (14" + 1" = 15"). The lengthwise distance between the inner weft filler strips is 20"; therefore, the cut length of the right and left border pieces is 21" (20" + 1" = 21").

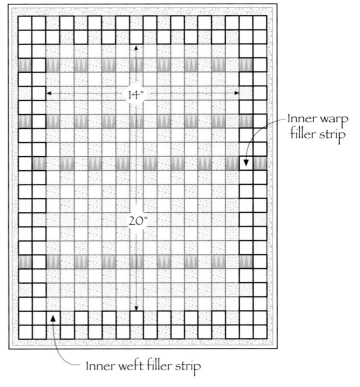

2. Prepare the inner border pieces. With the right side out, fold each piece in half lengthwise and press.

3. Pin the inner border pieces. Lay the woven and quilted top on a table, with the upper edge away from you. You'll add the inner border in a clockwise direction, beginning at the right edge.

With the folded edge toward the center, lay one of the side border pieces on the quilt top so that the fold is at the center of the first print strip. (If you quilted in the center of each strip, the fold should touch the stitching.) Make sure the border is equidistant from the upper and lower edges. Pin the border with the heads of the pins toward the outer edge.

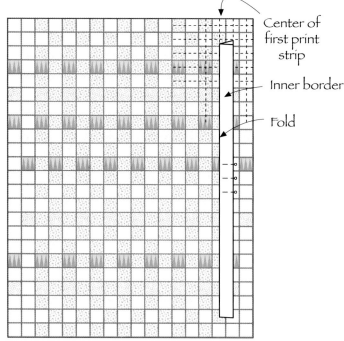

Center of first print strip

Inner border

Fold

At the lower edge of the quilt, pin one of the upper or lower border pieces in the same way, lapping the second piece over the first at the corner. Continue working around the quilt, pinning the remaining two pieces. At the upper right corner, lay the fourth border piece under the first one.

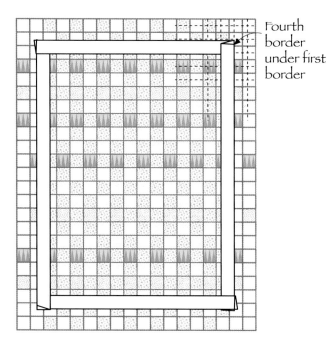

Fourth border under first border

Make sure that each inner border piece is on top at one end and under at the other end. Don't stitch the borders yet.

4. Prepare the outer border pieces. You'll need four pieces. Typically, the theme fabric is used for the outer border. The tropical print is used for the outer border on "Tropic Ice."

The cut width of the outer borders is equal to the finished width of the border (including the portion encased by the binding) plus ½" for the seam allowance used to stitch the border to the quilt top. The finished border width on "Tropic Ice," including the binding, is 2"; therefore, the cut width of the outer border pieces is 2½".

The cut length of the outer border pieces is equal to the finished width and length of the quilt. On "Tropic Ice," the cut length of the upper and lower borders is 17"; the cut length of the side borders is 23".

5. Using a rotary ruler and a marker, mark a stitching line on the wrong side ½" from one long edge of each border piece.

6. Pin the outer borders to the quilt. The outer borders will overlap each other in the same way as the inner borders. With the quilt flat and the upper edge away from you, begin at the right edge. Lay a long border piece, right side down, over the inner border, matching the raw edges. The outer border will cover the inner border and extend to the upper and lower edges of the quilt. Pin the border in place through all thicknesses.

7. Stitch the outer and inner borders. Sew along the marked stitching line through all thicknesses, beginning several inches below the inner border (2½" on "Tropic Ice") and stitching to the lower edge. Stitch slowly and let the machine pull the fabric through at a steady pace.

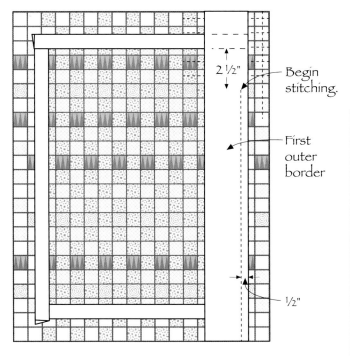

2 ½"

Begin stitching.

First outer border

½"

Flip the outer border so it's right side up and press. You've just applied two borders using only one seam!

8. Stitch the remaining borders. Move to the lower edge of the quilt and apply the lower border piece, lapping it over the first border. Add the third border in the same way.

When you add the fourth border to the upper edge, fold the unstitched section of the first border out of the way. Pin and stitch the fourth border all the way across the top.

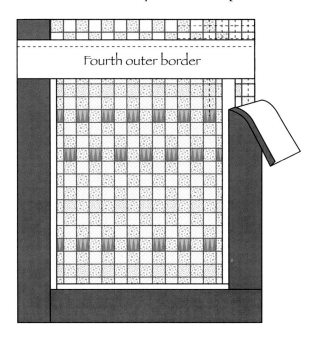

Fourth outer border

9. Finish stitching the first border. Press the fourth border, then return to the first border and stitch the unstitched section, lapping it over the fourth border.

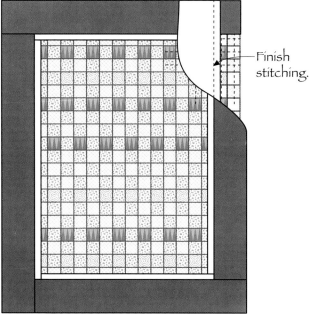

Finish stitching.

Attaching the Binding

The binding encases the raw edges and finishes the quilt. The binding for "Tropic Ice" is cut from the same fabric as the outer border. Binding a quilt with the border fabric keeps the center of interest on the woven area and does not detract from the inner border.

For woven and quilted projects, I use a single binding rather than the usual double-fold binding found on most quilts. I prefer the single binding because it's less bulky on a woven quilt top, which already has an extra layer of fabric.

For the most economical use of the fabric, cut the binding on the cross grain.

1. Determine the amount of binding. Measure the perimeter of the quilt and add approximately 15" to turn the corners and overlap at the start and finish. The perimeter of "Tropic Ice" measures 80"; therefore, the length of the binding is 95".

To determine the cut width of the binding, choose the finished width. Multiply that number by four and add ½" for the fabric that is lost in the turn of the folds. The cut width of the binding on "Tropic Ice" is 2½"; the finished width is ½".

2. Prepare the binding. Cut the ends of the binding pieces at a 45° angle and seam to make a long, continuous piece; press the seams open.

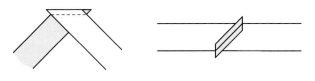

3. Pin and stitch the binding to the first edge. Begin at the upper right edge of the quilt, about 5" from the corner. Fold the end of the binding to form a 45° angle as shown. With the raw edges aligned, pin the binding to the outer edge of the quilt, being careful not to stretch the binding or the quilt.

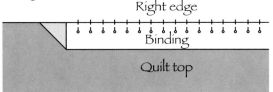

Using a ½"-wide seam allowance, stitch the binding. Stop ½" from the lower edge. Backstitch and clip the threads.

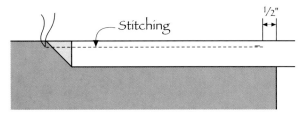

4. Form the mitered corners. Rotate the quilt one-quarter turn so that the edge with the sewn binding is at the top. Fold the binding straight up and away from the quilt to form a 45° angle at the corner. Finger-press the fold.

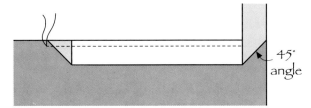

Hold the diagonal fold with your finger while you bring the binding straight down. The binding will form a fold even with the upper edge of the quilt. Pin; beginning at the top of the fold, stitch using a ½"-wide seam allowance. A mitered fold will form at the corner.

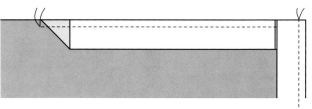

Continue stitching the binding. Stop the stitching ½" from the upper edge of the quilt.

5. Add the hanging sleeve. Cut a rectangle of backing fabric 10" wide and equal in length to the finished width of the quilt. The hanging sleeve for "Tropic Ice" is cut 10" x 17". Turn under 1" on each short end and press. Fold the rectangle in half lengthwise with the 1" folds to the inside. With raw edges aligned, center the sleeve at the top of the quilt and pin.

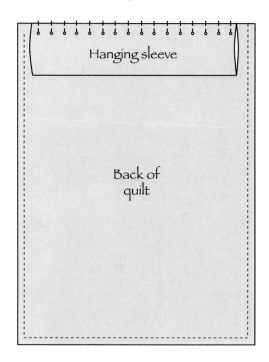

6. Finish stitching the binding. Stitch the remainder of the binding to the quilt, sewing the hanging sleeve at the same time. When you reach the starting point, overlap the binding beyond the beginning stitches; backstitch and clip the threads. Trim the excess binding on the diagonal.

7. Fold the binding to the back of the quilt and turn under the raw edge so that the fold just covers the stitching. Mitered corners will form automatically on the front. On the back, fold the miters in the opposite direction to reduce the bulk.

8. Slipstitch the binding to the back of the quilt. Make sure the stitches don't show on the front or the back. Hand stitch the folds in the mitered corners.

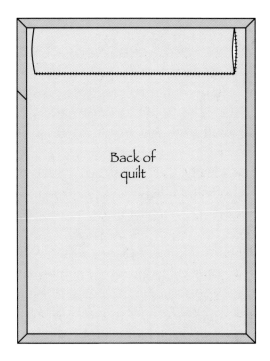

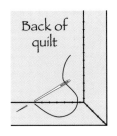

9. Finish attaching the sleeve. Hand stitch the lower edge and ends of the hanging sleeve to the back of the quilt.

10. Sign your work. Add a label with your name, date, and quilt title. Use a small square of fabric with the information written in permanent marking pen, or take the time to create a fancy hand- or machine-embroidered label. Stitch the label to the back of the quilt in the lower right corner.

Enjoy your quilt! Turn to the projects, beginning on page 34, for more ideas.

WOVEN & QUILTED PROJECTS

This section contains instructions for making the projects. Most of the projects call for warp and weft strips that are torn across the width of the fabric.

The "Materials" section of each project includes all the fabrics and notions you'll need to complete the project. Fabric requirements are based on 44"-wide fabric.

Before you tear or cut your strips, look carefully at the yardage chart to see the number and size of the pieces. To avoid running out of fabric, tear or cut the largest pieces or strips first. It also helps to sketch a cutting layout to see how to tear or cut the pieces most economically.

For best results, use only very lightweight polyester batting. See "Batting" on page 10 for specific guidelines.

It can't be said enough: Check the alignment of your warp and weft strips often. If the strips begin to wander, your finished weaving will be less than straight—and you will be less than pleased!

Finally, keep your weaving snug to prevent the batting from showing between the strips. It's especially important at the edges, where the border seams can separate the strips just enough to reveal the batting.

Use the woven and quilted process to make a variety of projects.

PEEK-A-BOO CATS

MATERIALS
44"-wide fabric

37" x 41"

2 yds. black-background print with cats or other decorative figures for backing, weft, and appliqués*

¼ yd. densely patterned, allover cat print or other print with no background for weft

⅞ yd. white-background stripe for warp and weft

1⅛ yds. black-background scatter print for warp and weft

¼ yd. bright pink solid for warp and weft

1¼ yds. black solid for border and hanging sleeve

⅝ yd. muslin or scrap fabric for filler strips

1¼ yds. very lightweight polyester batting

Quilting thread: smoky monofilament on the top and black poly/cotton in the bobbin

*You may need more or less fabric, depending on the size and spacing of the motifs for the border appliqués.

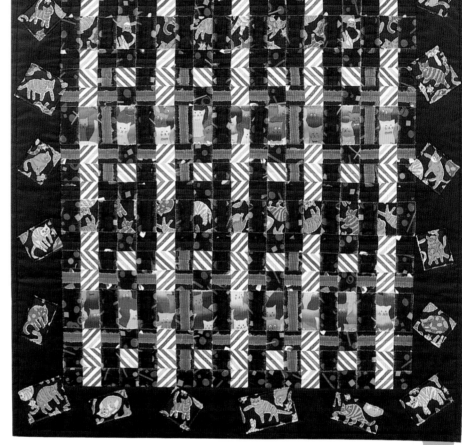

Peek-a-Boo Cats by Mary Anne Caplinger, 1994, Wilkesboro, North Carolina, 37" x 41". Treat your friends and family to a wall hanging that celebrates the playfulness of the cat. You can easily adapt this design to other theme prints.

Fabric	Used for	Number of Pieces	Size
Black-background cat print	Backing	1	39" x 43"
	Weft	2	2½" x 37"
	Appliqués	22	Varies
Densely patterned cat print	Weft	2	3" x 37"
Stripe	Warp (bias cut)	5	1½" x 41"
	Weft (bias cut)	5	1½" x 37"
Scatter print	Warp	14	1½" x 41"
	Weft	10	1½" x 37"
Bright pink	Warp	6	¾" x 11"
	Weft	4	¾" x 37"
Black solid	Border	2	5" x 42"
	Border	2	5" x 38"
	Binding	1	2½" x 160"
	Hanging sleeve	1	10" x 32"
Muslin	Warp	6	1½" x 41"
	Weft	6	1½" x 37"
Batting		1	38" x 42"

Peek-a-Boo Cats

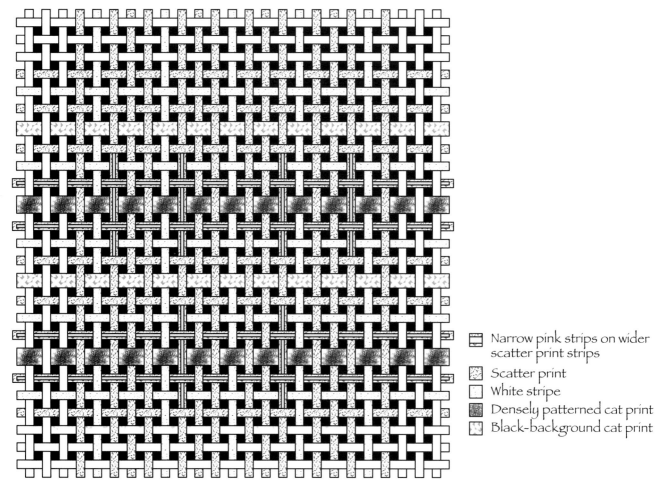

Narrow pink strips on wider scatter print strips
Scatter print
White stripe
Densely patterned cat print
Black-background cat print

DIRECTIONS

For complete instructions, refer to "The Woven and Quilted Process," beginning on page 19.

Weaving

1. Secure the backing and batting to your work surface; see step 4 of "Getting Started," page 20.

2. Prepare the strips; see "Preparing Strips from a Full Width of Fabric" on page 23. Lay the warp strips on the batting in the order shown in the weaving diagram.

NOTE

Each narrow pink warp strip is centered on a wider scatter print warp strip and the two strips are woven as one. A dot of fabric glue every few inches will hold the strips during weaving. The double warp strips do not extend to the edges; refer to the weaving diagram for placement.

---

3. Weave the weft strips, handling the double strips as you did on the warp; see "Weaving the Weft Strips" on page 24. Check the alignment every other row, using your rotary ruler or yardsticks.

4. Pin-baste the layers; see "Pin Basting," page 27.

Quilting

Quilt in the center of each warp and weft strip, except weft rows 7, 11, 15, and 19; see "Machine Quilting" on page 27. Leave these wide weft strips unstitched to emphasize the motifs.

Adding the Border

1. To attach the outer border, see steps 5–9 on pages 30–31, with these changes: Disregard the references to the inner border. Lay the right border, right side down, 4" from the outer right edge of the first filler strip; when you stitch this border using a ½"-wide seam allowance, the stitching should fall at the outer edge of the first print strip. Stitch, starting 7" from the upper edge.

2. Tear or cut squares for the appliqués, centering one cat motif in each square; fringe the edges. Arrange the appliqués randomly on the border and pin in place. Stitch carefully around the edge of each appliqué, just inside the fringe.

Attaching the Binding

1. Trim the outer edges of the quilt to the finished size, 37" x 41".

2. Attach the binding and the hanging sleeve; see "Attaching the Binding" on pages 31–33.

HOLIDAY HARMONIES

31½" x 34"

MATERIALS

44"-wide fabric

NOTE

All warp and weft strips are torn on the cross grain.

1¼ yds. light holiday print for background and inner border

1¼ yds. dark green holiday print for warp and weft, inner border, and outer border

1¼ yds. unbleached muslin for backing and sleeve

10 yds. red ribbon, ⅟₁₆" wide, for bows

1 yd. very lightweight polyester batting

41 assorted Christmas buttons and bells

Quilting thread: green metallic on the top and beige poly/cotton in the bobbin

Holiday Harmonies by Mary Anne Caplinger, 1994, Wilkesboro, North Carolina, 31½" x 34". This woven and quilted Christmas tree is one of the easiest holiday quilts you'll ever make! Start a collection of bell ornaments now and add a new one each year.

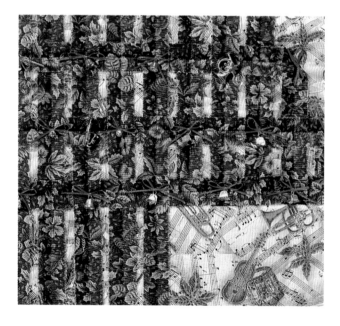

Small bells and bows decorate the "boughs."

Fabric	Used for	Number of Pieces	Size
Light print	Background	1	33" x 35½"
	Inner border	4	1¾" x 30"
Dark green print	Inner border	4	2¾" x 30"
	Outer border	4	4½" x 37"
	Warp	1	1" x 25"
		2	1" x 24"
		2	1" x 21½"
		2	1" x 14½"
		2	1" x 12"
		2	1" x 9½"
		2	1" x 7"
		2	1" x 4½"
	Weft	1	1" x 22"
		1	1" x 19½"
		1	1" x 17"
		1	1" x 14½"
		1	1" x 12"
		1	1" x 9½"
		1	1" x 7"
		1	1" x 4½"
Muslin	Backing	1	33" x 35½"
	Sleeve	1	10" x 27½"
Ribbon	Small bows	43	6" lengths
	Large bow	4	12" lengths
Batting		1	33" x 35½"

DIRECTIONS

For complete instructions, refer to "The Woven and Quilted Process," beginning on page 19.

Weaving

In this quilt, the warp and weft are spread on the background fabric. To keep your weaving straight, you'll lightly mark guidelines for the placement of the warp and weft strips.

1. Fold the background fabric in half lengthwise and press the crease; fold the fabric in half crosswise and press the crease. Unfold and gently smooth the fabric without losing the creases. Using chalk and your rotary ruler, mark the lengthwise and crosswise folds. Following the weaving diagram, measure and mark warp and weft guidelines on either side of the marked folds.

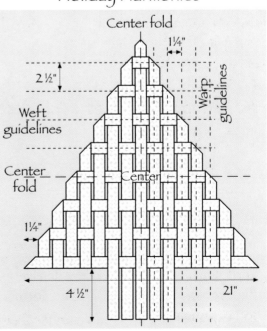

Holiday Harmonies

The warp guidelines are 1¼" apart; the weft guidelines are 2½" apart.

2. Secure the backing and batting to your work surface; see step 4 of "Getting Started" on page 20. Lay the marked background fabric on top of the batting and secure it with pins.

3. Prepare the strips; see "Preparing Strips from a Full Width of Fabric" on page 23. Fold the 25" warp strip in half to find the midpoint; crease or mark with a pin. Lay the warp strip over the center guideline, matching the midpoint of the strip to the center point on the background fabric; anchor the ends of the strip with pins. Lay the other warp strips over the warp guidelines as shown in the weaving diagram, anchoring the ends of the strips with pins.

4. Lay the weft strips over the weft guidelines as shown in the weaving diagram and weave; see "Weaving the Weft Strips" on page 24. Check the alignment and spacing after every row, using your rotary ruler or yardsticks.

5. Trim the end of each weft strip even with the end of each warp strip. Place the end of each warp strip over the end of each weft strip. Hold the edges of the strips together and turn under to form a diagonal fold as shown.

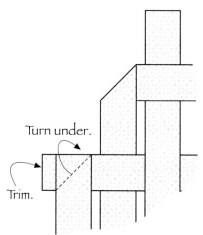

Turn under.

Trim.

6. Trim the center warp strip at the top and turn under the corners to form the tree tip; pin.

7. Turn under ½" on each warp strip that forms the tree trunk and pin; the quilting stitches will secure the ends.

8. At the lower edge of the tree, trim the warp strips that fall under the last weft strip so that the ends are hidden. Fold the warp strips that fall on top of the last weft strip under the strip and pin. Check the alignment.

9. Pin-baste the layers; see "Pin Basting," page 27.

Quilting

Quilt in the center of each warp and weft strip; see "Machine Quilting" on pages 27–28. Pull the top threads to the back and tie; clip the threads.

Adding the Borders

This quilt features two narrow inner borders.

1. Fold 1 dark inner border piece and 1 light inner border piece in half lengthwise and press. Lay the light inner border piece on top of the dark inner border piece, matching the raw edges. Treat these 2 pieces as 1 border unit.

2. On the right edge of the quilt, measure 3⅜" from the edge and mark with pins. With the folded edges toward the center, pin the border unit to the quilt so that the inner fold just touches the line of pins. Make sure the border unit is equidistant from the upper and lower edges.

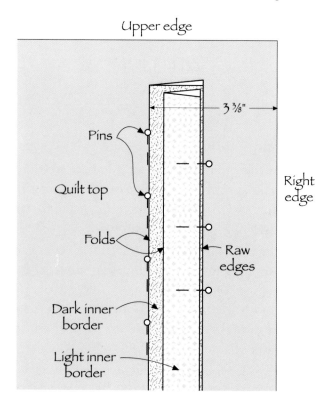

Upper edge

Pins

Quilt top

Folds

Dark inner border

Light inner border

3⅜"

Right edge

Raw edges

3. At the lower edge of the quilt, pin a border unit in the same way, lapping it over the first border unit at the corner. Continue working around the quilt, pinning the remaining two border units. At the upper right corner, lay the fourth border unit under the first border unit. Trim the ends of the upper and lower border units to fit. Don't stitch the borders yet.

4. The outer border seems wider than necessary. That's because the outer border serves as both border and binding. To attach the outer border, see steps 5–9 on pages 30–31, with the following change: after you stitch the upper border, prepare and pin the hanging sleeve; see step 5 on page 32. (Note that the cut length of the hanging sleeve, 27½", is shorter than the finished width of the quilt. That's to allow you to finish stitching the first border without catching the sleeve.) Using a ½"-wide seam allowance, stitch the hanging sleeve to the upper edge, keeping the upper and right borders free. Finish stitching the right border. Trim the upper and lower borders to fit.

Finishing

1. Turn the extra 1½" of outer border fabric all the way to the back of the quilt on the right and left edges; turn under ¾" and pin. Repeat on the upper and lower edges. Fold square, rather than mitered, corners as shown. Slipstitch the binding to the back of the quilt.

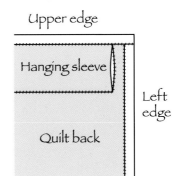

2. For the large bow at the top of the tree, hold four 12" lengths of ribbon together and tie a bow. Thread a bell onto each ribbon tail; tie a double knot and trim. Hand sew the bow to the top of the tree.

3. With each of sixteen 6" lengths of ribbon, make a small bow. Hand sew the bows to the ends of the "boughs."

4. With each remaining length of ribbon, thread a bell or button onto one end; tie a bow. Sew the bows at the intersections of the warp and weft strips. Or, sew the bells and buttons to the tree; make separate bows and sew them above the ornaments.

Christmas Tree Ornaments by Mary Anne Caplinger, 1994, Wilkesboro, North Carolina. Miniature woven and quilted ornaments enliven a traditional holiday tree. The stocking, bell, and mini-medallion quilt are woven with strips of Poppanna, a Finnish "yarn" that is actually ⅜"-wide bias-cut fabric strips on a roll. See Resources on page 79.

See Resources on page 79.

Beginner

MINI-MEDALLION QUILT

4⅛" x 5"

Small piece of red solid for backing
¼ yd. green print for binding
Small piece of novelty Christmas print for center medallion
1¾ yds. red Poppanna, color #5, for warp and weft

MATERIALS

44"-wide fabric

2½ yds. white Poppanna, color #85, for warp and weft
2½ yds. red ribbon, ¹⁄₁₆" wide, for bows
Small piece of very lightweight polyester batting
Quilting thread: white and red poly/cotton on the top and in the bobbin
4 small bells, ¼" diameter

Fabric	Used for	Number of Pieces	Size
Red solid	Backing	1	5" x 6"
Green print	Binding	1	1¼" x 25"
Novelty print	Medallion	1	2" x 2¾"
Red Poppanna	Warp	4	6" lengths
	Weft	4	5" lengths
	Weft	4	1¾" lengths
White Poppanna	Warp	6	6" lengths
	Warp	2	1¾" lengths
	Weft	6	5" lengths
	Weft	6	1¾" lengths
Ribbon	Bows	6	6" lengths
	Loop and bows	2	24" lengths
Batting		1	5" x 6"

DIRECTIONS

Weaving

1. Secure the backing and batting to your work surface with pins.

2. Lay the warp strips on the batting as shown in the weaving diagram, anchoring the ends of the strips with pins.

3. Weave the first 4 weft strips, alternating white and red as shown in the weaving diagram; see "Weaving the Weft Strips" on page 24. Handle the bias-cut Poppanna carefully because it stretches easily.

4. After the fourth weft row, slip the center medallion under the warp and weft strips and pin in place. Continue to weave the short rows on either side of the medallion. After the ninth weft row, continue to weave full rows. Check the alignment of the strips, using your rotary ruler.

5. Pin-baste the layers; see "Pin Basting," page 27.

Mini-Medallion Quilt

☐ Red   ☐ White

Quilting

Quilt in the center of each warp and weft strip, changing the thread color to match the dominant color in each row. Do not stitch over the center medallion.

Finishing

1. Trim the outer edges so the miniquilt measures 4⅛" x 5". Using a ¼"-wide seam allowance, attach the binding; see "Attaching the Binding" on pages 31–33.

2. To make the hanging loop, hold two 24" lengths of ribbon together and fold in half. Measure 5" from the fold on one side and make a small bow. Repeat on the other side.

3. Sew the bows at the upper corners of the miniquilt. Thread a bell onto each ribbon tail; tie a double knot and trim.

4. From each of the 6" lengths of ribbon, tie a small bow and hand sew it to the quilt. Space the bows in a circle around the medallion.

STOCKING

7³⁄₈" long

MATERIALS
44"-wide fabric

1 fat quarter red solid for back of stocking, backing, and binding
3½ yds. dark green Poppanna, color #50, for warp
1⅝ yds. red Poppanna, color #5, for weft
1¾ yds. white Poppanna, color #85, for weft

2 yds. red ribbon, ¹⁄₁₆" wide
¼ yd. very lightweight polyester batting
Quilting thread: gold metallic on the top and gold rayon in the bobbin
4 small bells, ¼" diameter
Tracing paper, 6" x 12"

Fabric	Used for	Number of Pieces	Size
Red solid	Back of stocking	1	6" x 8"
	Backing	2	6" x 12"
	Binding (bias cut)	1	1½" x 20"
Green Poppanna	Warp	14	8" lengths
Red Poppanna	Weft	9	6" lengths
White Poppanna	Weft	10	6" lengths
Ribbon	Loop and bow	2	1 yd. lengths
Batting		2	6" x 10"

DIRECTIONS

Weaving

1. Lay 1 of the red backing pieces on your work surface and lay the batting on top, matching the lower edges. At the upper edge, the backing will be 2" longer than the batting. You will later trim and fold this extra fabric to make the cuff. Secure the batting and backing to your work surface with pins.

2. Cut the warp and weft strips specified in the yardage chart. Lay the green warp strips on the batting as shown in the weaving diagram, anchoring the ends of the strips with pins.

3. Weave the weft strips, alternating white and red as shown in the weaving diagram; see "Weaving the Weft Strips" on page 24. Handle the bias-cut Poppanna carefully because it stretches easily. Check the alignment, using your rotary ruler.

4. Pin-baste the layers; see "Pin Basting," page 27.

Stocking

■ Green   ☐ Red   ☐ White

Quilting

Quilt a diagonal grid, with the threads crossing in the center of every other red square, or quilt a pattern of your choice.

Assembling the Stocking

1. To make the back of the stocking, layer the remaining 2 pieces of red fabric with the remaining piece of batting in between. Align the 3 pieces at the lower edge.

2. Mark a diagonal grid to match the one on the front of the stocking; pin-baste and quilt.

3. Trace the stocking pattern on page 48 and cut it out. Lay the pattern on top of the woven and quilted piece and mark the outline. Carefully cut out the stocking. Trim the batting 1½" above the woven area. Trim the backing 3" above the woven area. Repeat for the back of the stocking.

4. Lay the back of the stocking, right side down, on your work surface. Place the front of the stocking on top, right side up. Pin the outer edges, leaving the upper edges free; stitch, using a scant ¼"-wide seam allowance.

5. Begin attaching the binding at the upper right edge of the weaving (not the upper edge of the stocking). With right sides together and raw edges aligned, pin the binding to the edge of the stocking. Ease the binding around the outside curve of the toe and heel and gently stretch the binding around the front inside curve. Using a ¼"-wide seam allowance, stitch the binding to the edge of the stocking, ending at the upper left edge of the weaving.

6. Fold the binding to the back and turn under the raw edge so that the fold just covers the stitching. Slipstitch the binding to the back of the stocking.

7. Fold the upper edge of the stocking over the batting. Fold once more to create a 1½"-wide cuff.

Finishing

1. To make the hanging loop and bow, hold the two 1-yard lengths of ribbon together and fold in half. Measure 7" from the fold and make an overhand knot.

2. Separate the tails into 2 groups of 2 ribbons and tie a bow close to the overhand knot. Thread a bell onto each ribbon tail; tie a double knot and trim. Sew the bow to the cuff.

BELL

4³/₄" x 5³/₄"

MATERIALS

44"-wide fabric

¼ yd. red solid for back of bell and binding
¼ yd. green print or solid for backing
1 yd. dark green Poppanna, color #50,
 for warp and weft
4 yds. red Poppanna, color #5, for warp and weft
1¼ yds. white Poppanna, color #85, for warp
 and weft

3 yds. red ribbon, ¹/₁₆" wide
¼ yd. very lightweight polyester batting
Quilting thread: gold metallic on the top and
 gold rayon in the bobbin
4 bells, ½" diameter
Tracing paper, 6" x 7"

Fabric	Used for	Number of Pieces	Size
Red solid	Back of bell	1	6" x 7"
	Binding (bias cut)	1	1¼" x 11½"
		2	1¼" x 7"
Green print or solid	Backing	2	6" x 7"
Green Poppanna	Warp	2	6" lengths
	Weft	2	7" lengths
Red Poppanna	Warp	10	6" lengths
	Weft	10	7" lengths
White Poppanna	Warp	4	6" lengths
	Weft	2	7" lengths
Ribbon	Loop and bow	2	1 yd. lengths
	Ringer	2	12" lengths
Batting		2	6" x 7"

Bell

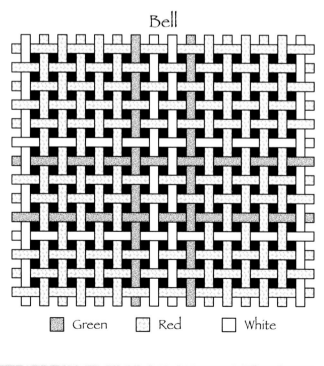

■ Green   ▨ Red   ☐ White

DIRECTIONS

Weaving

1. Secure 1 piece of green backing and 1 piece of batting to your work surface with pins.

2. Cut the warp and weft strips specified in the yardage chart. Lay the warp strips on the batting in the order shown in the weaving diagram, anchoring the ends of the strips with pins.

3. Weave the weft strips, alternating red, white, and green as shown in the weaving diagram; see "Weaving the Weft Strips" on page 24. Handle the bias-cut Poppanna carefully because it stretches easily. Check the alignment, using your rotary ruler.

4. Pin-baste the layers; see "Pin Basting," page 27.

Quilting

Quilt a ⅞" diagonal grid, or quilt a pattern of your choice.

Assembling the Bell

1. To make the back of the bell, layer the remaining pieces of red and green solids with the remaining piece of batting in between.

2. Mark a diagonal grid to match the one on the woven piece; pin-baste and quilt.

3. Trace half of the bell pattern on page 48; flip the tracing paper and trace the other half. Cut out the pattern. Lay the pattern on top of the woven piece and mark the outline. Carefully cut out the woven bell. Repeat for the back of the bell.

4. With right sides together and raw edges aligned, pin 1 short piece of binding to the lower edge of the woven bell. Stitch the binding, using a ¼"-wide seam allowance.

5. Fold the binding to the inside and turn under the raw edge so that the fold just covers the stitching. Slipstitch the binding to the bell. Repeat on the back of the bell. Trim the ends of the binding.

6. Lay the back of the bell, right side down, on your work surface. Place the woven bell, right side up, on top. Pin the outer edges, leaving the lower edges free. Stitch, using a scant ¼"-wide seam allowance.

7. Attach the remaining piece of binding to the outer edge, folding under the ends at the start and finish.

Finishing

1. To make the hanging loop and bow, hold the two 1-yard lengths of ribbon together and fold them in half. Measure 7" from the fold and make an overhand knot.

Separate the tails into 2 groups of 2 ribbons and tie a bow close to the overhand knot. Set aside.

2. To make the ringer, thread a bell onto each end of two 12" pieces of ribbon; tie a double knot and trim. Fold these pieces of ribbon in half.

Thread a hand sewing needle with a double length of red thread knotted at the end. From the outside, pierce the top of the bell at the center and pull the needle and thread through the inside of the bell. Drape the folded ribbons over the thread.

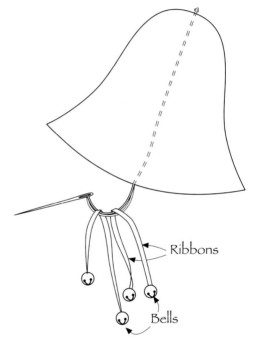

Bring the needle through the center of the bell to the outside, close to the point of entry.

Hold the bell so it hangs down and adjust the ribbons. Pull the thread tight and take a small stitch to secure the ribbons. Do not cut the thread.

3. Position the hanging loop and bow at the top of the bell. With the same needle and thread, take a few stitches to secure the bow. Cut the thread. Trim the ribbon tails.

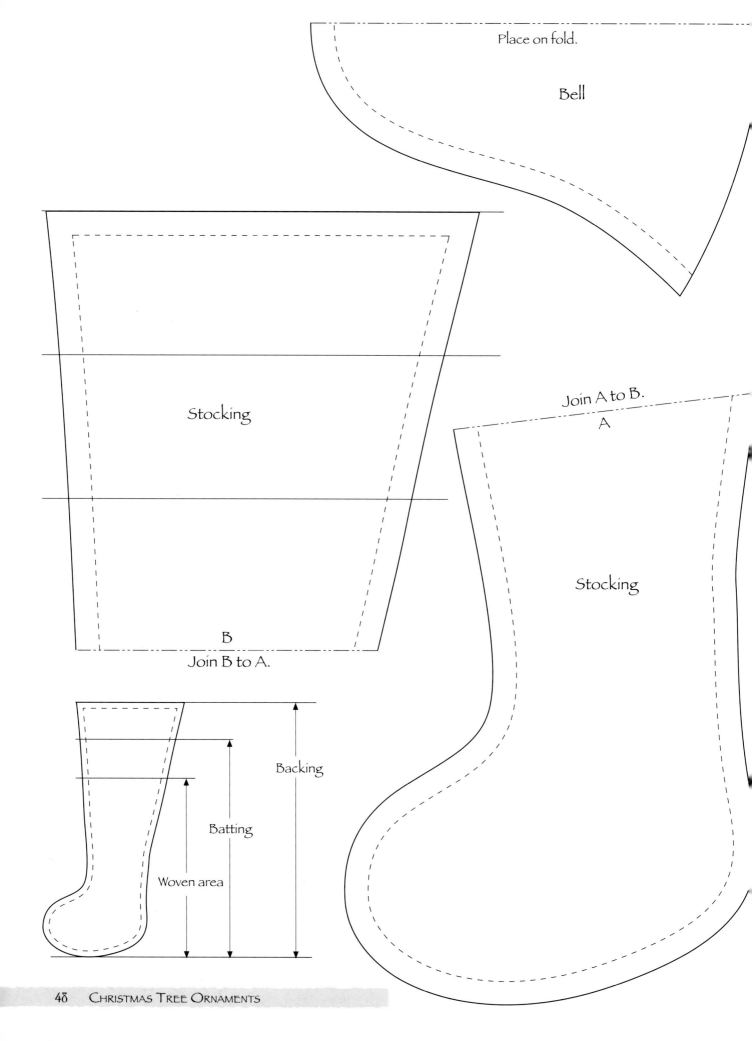

Place on fold.

Bell

Stocking

Join A to B.
A

Join B to A.
B

Stocking

Backing

Batting

Woven area

PRICKLY PEAR SALSA

MATERIALS
44"-wide fabric

NOTE

The warp and weft strips are torn on the cross grain. Each block contains at least one warp or one weft strip of the theme fabric; the other warp and weft strips are distributed randomly for a scrap-quilt look.

2 yds. large-scale print for warp, weft, outer border, back sashing, binding, and optional hanging sleeve

¼ yd. dark print for inner border

¼ yd. each of 16 or more coordinating prints for warp, weft, and front sashing

1 yd. very lightweight polyester batting

Quilting thread: assorted coordinating colors on the top and in the bobbin

Prickly Pear Salsa by Mary Anne Caplinger, 1994, Wilkesboro, North Carolina, 27" x 27". This small reversible quilt is constructed in modules, similar to the quilt-as-you-go technique. It's a great project for small spaces or small blocks of time. Assembling the blocks and sashing is a little like putting together the pieces of a puzzle.

Fabric	Used for	Number of Pieces	Size
Large-scale print	Outer border (front and back)	8	3½" x 24½"
	Sashing (back)	8	2" x 10¾"
	Sashing (back)	8	2" x 5¼"
	Sashing center square	1	2" x 2"
	Binding	1	2½" x 120"
	Outer warp and weft*	Varies	1¼" x 5¼"
	Inner warp and weft*	Varies	1" x 5¼"
	Perimeter warp and weft*	Varies	2" x 5¼"
	Hanging sleeve (optional)	1	10" x 23"
Dark print	Inner border	4	2" x 22½"
16 coordinating prints	Backing	1 each	5¼" x 5¼"
	Outer warp and weft*	Varies	1¼" x 5¼"
	Inner warp and weft*	Varies	1" x 5¼"
	Perimeter warp and weft*	Varies	2" x 5¼"
	Sashing (front)**	8 total	2" x 10¾"
	Sashing (front)**	8 total	2" x 5¼"
	Sashing center square**	1	2" x 2"
Batting	Batting (blocks)	16	5¼" x 5¼"
	Batting (borders)	4	3½" x 24½"
	Batting (sashing)	8	2" x 5¼"
	Batting (sashing)	8	2" x 10¾"

*Tear a variety of strips 1", 1¼", and 2" wide.

**Refer to the photo to cut the front sashing correctly.

When pieced, the strips should appear to be continuous and woven.

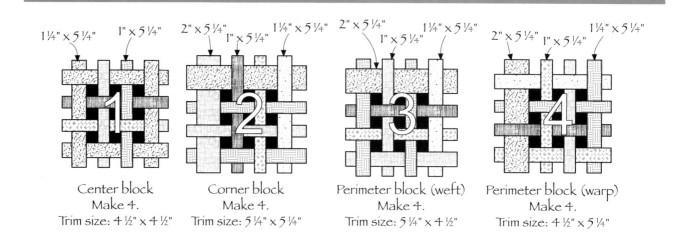

1¼" x 5¼"   1" x 5¼"

Center block
Make 4.
Trim size: 4½" x 4½"

2" x 5¼"   1" x 5¼"   1¼" x 5¼"

Corner block
Make 4.
Trim size: 5¼" x 5¼"

2" x 5¼"   1" x 5¼"   1¼" x 5¼"

Perimeter block (weft)
Make 4.
Trim size: 5¼" x 4½"

2" x 5¼"   1" x 5¼"   1¼" x 5¼"

Perimeter block (warp)
Make 4.
Trim size: 4½" x 5¼"

DIRECTIONS

For complete instructions, refer to "The Woven and Quilted Process," beginning on page 19.

Weaving

The quilt consists of 16 reversible blocks that you join after they are woven and quilted. Each block is composed of 4 warp and 4 weft strips. The warp and weft strips that touch the sashing and the border are wider to provide for seam allowances. Once you add the sashing and borders, all of the strips appear to be 1" wide.

The blocks are divided into 4 groups — 4 center blocks, 4 corner blocks, 4 perimeter warp blocks, and 4 perimeter weft blocks.

1. Secure a piece of 5¼" x 5¼" backing, right side down, and 5¼" x 5¼" batting to your work surface with pins.

2. Prepare the strips; see "Preparing Strips from a Full Width of Fabric" on page 23. Be sure to tear a variety of strip widths from each co-ordinating print as specified in the yardage chart.

3. Begin with the center blocks. Lay 4 warp strips — one 1¼" outer strip, two 1" inner strips, and one 1¼" outer strip as shown in the weaving diagrams on the opposite page.

4. Weave the weft strips in the same sequence as the warp; see "Weaving the Weft Strips" on page 24. Using a variety of strips, weave a total of 4 center blocks.

5. Pin-baste the layers of each block as soon as you finish weaving; see "Pin Basting" on page 27.

6. Weave and pin-baste 4 corner blocks, 4 perimeter weft blocks, and 4 perimeter warp blocks as shown in the weaving diagrams. Pay careful attention to the widths of the strips.

7. Arrange the blocks as shown below.

Quilting

1. The quilting pattern consists of diagonal lines that change direction from one horizontal row of blocks to the next; see "Machine Quilting" on pages 27–28.

2. Quilt the blocks and press lightly.

3. Trim each block to the size indicated in the weaving diagrams.

Assembling the Blocks

1. Trim the sashing pieces to the lengths needed as you assemble the quilt top. Place the sashing pieces between the blocks as shown below so you can easily see how the quilt fits together. The blocks, sashing, and borders are constructed in a variation of the quilt-as-you-go method.

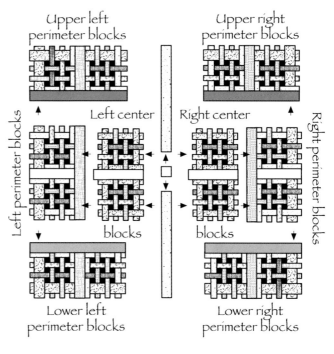

Upper left perimeter blocks

Upper right perimeter blocks

Left perimeter blocks

Left center   Right center

blocks   blocks

Right perimeter blocks

Lower left perimeter blocks

Lower right perimeter blocks

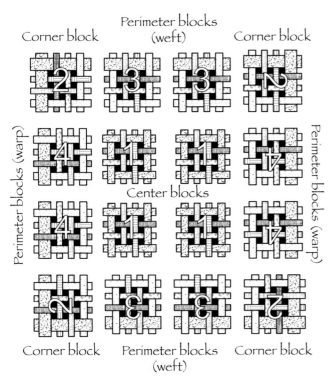

Corner block   Perimeter blocks (weft)   Corner block

Perimeter blocks (warp)

Center blocks

Perimeter blocks (warp)

Corner block   Perimeter blocks (weft)   Corner block

2. Begin with the upper left perimeter blocks. To apply the first 5¼" sashing strip to the right edge of the block, layer the pieces in this order, starting with the bottom layer: the batting strip; the back sashing strip, right side up; the woven and quilted block, right side up; and the front sashing strip, right side down.

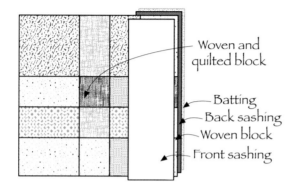

Make sure to attach the sashing pieces so that they appear to be continuous and woven when the quilt top is assembled; refer to the photo on page 49.

Using a ¼"-wide seam allowance, stitch the layers. Trim batting from seam allowance.

3. With right sides together, stitch the remaining long edge of the front sashing to the second block. Trim ¼" from the long unstitched edge of the batting and tuck it under the seam allowances. Turn under ¼" on the long edge of the back sashing; slipstitch to back of second block.

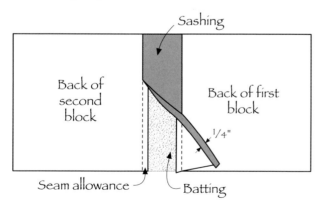

4. Attach the 5¼" sashing pieces to the remaining pairs of perimeter blocks as shown in the layout.

5. Attach 5¼" sashing pieces to center blocks.

6. Using the same procedure, attach the 10¾" sashing pieces to the two-block perimeter units.

7. Sew the left center unit to the left perimeter unit. Sew this completed unit to the upper left and lower left perimeter units. Repeat on the other side.

8. Sew the center sashing square to the remaining long sashing pieces. To make the sashing appear woven, cut this center square from the same fabric used for the sashing on either side of the square.

9. Sew the vertical center sashing to the left half of the quilt, then to the right half. Lightly press the quilt top.

Adding the Borders

1. Trim the outer edges to square the quilt top.

2. With the right side out, fold each inner border strip in half lengthwise and press.

3. Begin on the right edge of the quilt. With the folded edge of the border strip toward the center and the long raw edges aligned, pin the border strip to the quilt. The fold should fall at the middle of the outer strip.

4. At the lower edge, pin the next border strip to the quilt, lapping the right end over the first border strip. Working in a clockwise direction, pin the remaining border strips. At the upper edge, lay the fourth border strip under the first border strip at the right corner.

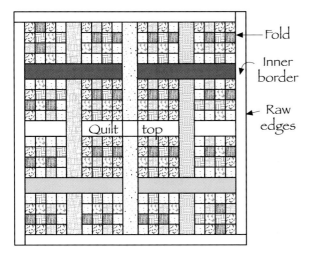

5. Pin the outer border to the quilt as you did the sashing, making a sandwich (from the bottom) with the batting, the back outer border, the quilt, the inner border, and the front outer border. (In the illustration below, the pieces are spread for clarity.)

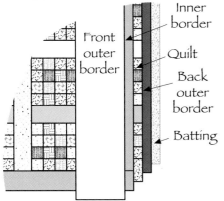

Beginning at the lower right edge of the quilt, align the raw edges of the borders and batting with the edge of the quilt; pin. The border will extend above the upper edge of the quilt.

6. Begin stitching 3" from the upper edge, using a ¼"-wide seam allowance.

7. Trim the batting from the seam allowance and flip the borders out. Smooth the layers and pin the edges.

8. Repeat the procedure at the lower edge of the quilt, lapping the lower border over the right border at the corner. Repeat for the left and upper borders.

9. At the upper right corner, finish attaching the first border.

Attaching the Binding

Attach the binding and hanging sleeve (optional); see "Attaching the Binding" on pages 31–33.

ANEMONE VEST

Anemone Vest by Karen James Swing, 1994, Boone, North Carolina. Spring-flowering anemones in fresh shades of blue and lavender frame the neckline of this vest. The blue and white fabrics used to weave the checkerboard front are hand stamped.

MATERIALS

44"-wide fabric
Other sizes may require more or less fabric and batting.

NOTE

The warp and weft strips are cut on the straight grain.

Vest pattern without darts

1½ yds. medium blue solid, hand stamped, or the yardage required for vest fronts and back; see pattern

¾ yd. white muslin, hand stamped, or yardage required for vest fronts; see pattern

¾ yd. white muslin, or yardage required for vest backing; see pattern

½ yd. large floral print for appliqués and binding

¾ yd. very lightweight polyester batting, or yardage required for entire vest; see pattern

Quilting thread: medium blue poly/cotton on the top and in the bobbin

Tools for hand stamping fabric include acrylic fabric paint, a carved eraser, and a felt stamp pad.

Fabric	Used for	Number of Pieces	Size
Blue solid	Back of vest	1	19" x 21"*
	Warp (cut)	25	1" x 22"
	Seam facing	2	1" x 8"
	Seam facing	2	1" x 5"
White muslin (stamped)	Weft (cut)	22	1" x 25"
White muslin	Backing (vest back)	1	19" x 21"*
	Backing (vest front)	1	22" x 25"*
Floral print	Appliqués	Approx. 8	Varies
	Binding (bias cut)	1	2" x 95"
	Binding (bias cut)	2	2" x 30"
Batting		1	19" x 21"*
		1	22" x 25"*

*Or a piece large enough to accommodate your pattern.

Anemone Vest

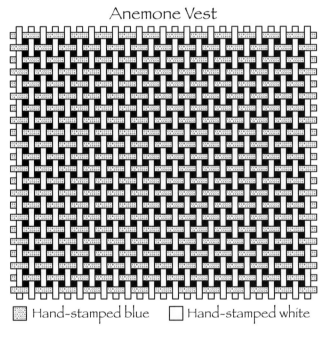

▨ Hand-stamped blue　　☐ Hand-stamped white

DIRECTIONS

For complete instructions, refer to "The Woven and Quilted Process," beginning on page 19.

Weaving

To match the weft rows on the front of the vest, you'll weave and quilt one large piece, then cut out the vest fronts.

1. Secure the backing and batting to your work surface; see step 4 of "Getting Started," page 20.

2. Using your rotary cutter and ruler, cut the warp and weft strips on the straight grain. Lay the warp strips on the batting in the order shown in the weaving diagram; anchor the ends with pins.

3. Weave the weft strips in the order shown in the weaving diagram; see "Weaving the Weft Strips" on page 24. Check the alignment every other row, using your rotary ruler or yardsticks.

4. Pin-baste the layers; see "Pin Basting," page 27.

Quilting

1. For the woven pieces, quilt in the center of each warp and weft strip; see "Machine Quilting" on pages 27–28.

2. For the vest back, mark a 1" straight grid on the hand-stamped blue fabric. Layer the muslin backing, the batting, and the blue fabric. Pin-baste the layers and quilt.

Assembling the Vest

1. Lightly press the quilted pieces. Lay the back pattern piece on the quilted back and mark; cut out the back.

2. Mark the vest front pattern along the outside edge every 5" to help match the weft rows. Lay the pattern piece on the left side and mark; cut out the left front. Turn the pattern over and mark the right side, matching the edge marks to the weft rows; cut out the right front.

3. Cut the appliqués for the vest front from the floral print, following the outline of the flowers. Select a variety of shapes and sizes.

4. Place flowers at the neckline of the vest fronts, with larger flowers in the center and smaller ones tapering to the edges. Experiment with the placement until the arrangement is pleasing. Stitch flowers ⅛" from raw edges.

5. Sew the shoulder seams and side seams, using a ⅝"-wide seam allowance or the seam allowance called for in your pattern. Trim the seams and press them open.

6. Turn under ¼" along each long edge of one seam facing and press. Pin the facing over the corresponding seam allowance; hand stitch. Repeat with the other facings.

Attaching the Binding

1. Cut the ends of the binding pieces at a 45° angle and seam to make the lengths required; press the seams open.

2. Begin attaching binding at the lower edge of the left side seam. Turn under ¼" at one end of the bias strip and press. With right sides together and raw edges aligned, pin binding to the vest.

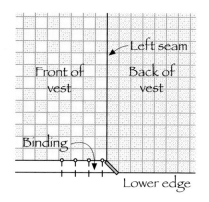

3. Stitch the binding to the vest front, back, and neckline, using a ⅜"-wide seam allowance. When you reach the starting point, overlap the binding 2" beyond the beginning stitches; backstitch and clip the threads.

4. Fold the binding to the inside of the vest, turning under ⅜" so that the fold just covers the stitching. Slipstitch the binding in place.

5. Attach the binding to the armholes, beginning and ending at the side seams.

HAND PRINTING THE FABRIC

Stamping fabric is fun and easy to do, and you'll love the custom look it lends to a woven and quilted garment. A design with a few straight lines or gentle curves creates an interesting repeat pattern. Select a soft rubber eraser and use a craft knife to carve the design, or use a commercial rubber stamp.

You'll also need a paper plate, a 5" x 5" piece of white felt, a smaller piece of white cotton fabric, fabric paint, and a plastic spoon.

1. Place the white felt on the paper plate. Cover the felt with the piece of white fabric.

2. Put ½ tsp. of fabric paint in the center of the cotton and work it in with the back of the spoon.

To test the stamp, press it firmly on the pad, then press it on a piece of scrap fabric.

3. Draw light pencil lines on your fabric or use a rotary ruler as a guide to keep the rows of printing straight and parallel.

4. Stamp your fabric, adding more paint to the pad as necessary. Don't worry if the paint is slightly uneven; color variation is a natural characteristic of hand printing.

5. Clean the stamp with a damp cloth.

6. Allow the fabric to dry overnight; heat-set according to the manufacturer's instructions.

CIRCLES OF VIOLET

MATERIALS

44"-wide fabric
20"-wide fusible interfacing
Smaller sizes may require less fabric.

NOTE

The weft strips are cut on the
cross grain,
folded in thirds, and pressed.

Vest pattern without darts
3 yds. large-scale purple print for
    vest back, weft, and binding
1½ yds. fusible interfacing
44 yds. purple ribbon, ⅛" wide,
    for warp
1 yd. magenta solid for lining
Small scraps of green prints or
    solids and felt for corsage
Pin back for corsage

*Circles of Violet by Fran Ginthwain, 1994,
Conover, North Carolina. Narrow purple ribbon replaces
fabric warp strips in this vest variation. The weft strips are
folded in thirds, creating a three-dimensional effect.*

*A yo-yo corsage embellished
with ribbons and buttons adds
a fanciful touch.*

Fabric	Used for	Number of Pieces	Size
Purple print	Vest back	1	Varies*
	Weft	136	¾" x 14"
	Binding (bias cut)	1	1¾" x 104"
	Binding (bias cut)	2	1¾" x 32"
Fusible interfacing	Front underlining	2	Varies*
Ribbon	Warp	50	28" lengths
	Bow	4	24" lengths
Magenta solid	Lining	3	Varies*
Green solid	Corsage leaves	3	4" diameter circles
Felt	Corsage base	1	2½" diameter circle

*You'll need a piece large enough to accommodate your pattern.

Circles of Violet

DIRECTIONS

For complete instructions, refer to "The Woven and Quilted Process," beginning on page 19.

Weaving

This vest doesn't require batting between the woven front and the lining. The weft strips are folded in thirds, creating a slightly puffy look.

1. You must weave the vest fronts separately because the fusible interfacing is narrow. Measure the vest front pattern piece at its longest and widest points. Add 3" to the length and width for the cut size of each piece of interfacing.

2. Secure the interfacing, fusible side up, to your work surface. Tape or pin the lengths of ribbon to the interfacing, spacing them ½" apart.

3. Using your rotary cutter and ruler, cut the weft strips on the cross grain. Fold one long edge of each strip ¼" to the wrong side; press. Fold the other long edge over the first edge and press. Repeat for all the weft strips.

4. Weave with the folded weft strips, cut edge down, as shown in the weaving diagram; see "Weaving the Weft Strips" on page 24. Check the alignment every other row, using your rotary ruler or yardsticks.

5. Press the woven piece to fuse the strips to the interfacing, following the manufacturer's instructions.

Quilting

Because the weft is fused to the interfacing, it's not necessary to quilt the vest fronts. If you wish to do decorative stitching on the fronts, mark the lines and pin-baste. Stitch slowly and carefully to prevent the folded strips from getting caught under the presser foot.

Assembling the Vest

1. Lay the pattern piece on the left front and mark the outer edges. Pin-baste; machine stitch on the marked line to hold the weft in place. Flip the pattern and repeat for the right front. Cut out the fronts just outside the stitching lines.

2. Sew the shoulder seams and side seams, using a ⅝"-wide seam allowance or the seam allowance called for in your pattern. Press the seam allowances to the back.

3. Cut out front and back lining pieces and sew the shoulder seams and side seams. Press seam allowances open. With wrong sides together, pin the lining to the vest at all the raw edges.

Attaching the Binding

See "Attaching the Binding" on page 56, with this important change: stitch the binding to the vest using a ¼"-wide seam allowance.

YO-YO CORSAGE

1. For the yo-yo flowers, cut 7 circles from the lining and print fabrics in the following sizes: 2 circles with a 4" diameter, 2 circles with a 3" diameter, and 3 circles with a 2" diameter.

2. Thread a hand sewing needle with a double strand of thread. Leaving a 4" tail, knot the ends. Sew with a running stitch ⅛" from the edge of each circle. Pull the threads tightly to gather the fabric in the center; flatten the gathered circle and tie the thread tails. Sew a button in the center of each yo-yo.

3. For the leaves, cut 3 circles with a 4" diameter from the green solid and print scraps. Fold each circle in half, then in half again. Sew with a running stitch ⅛" from the raw edges. Gather slightly and take a few stitches to hold the gathers.

4. Cut a 2½" felt circle for the base. Hold four 24" lengths of ribbon together; tie a bow with 6" loops. Sew or glue bow to center of base.

5. Arrange the leaves and yo-yo flowers on the base and sew or glue in place. Sew or glue a pin back to the back of the base.

GARDEN MEDLEY

Garden Medley by Mary Anne Caplinger, 1994, Wilkesboro, North Carolina. A variety of woven and quilted accessories in cool, contemporary greens and violets enhance a decorating scheme.

*Curtain Tieback by Mary Anne Caplinger,
1994, Wilkesboro, North Carolina, 3" x 30". A length
of grosgrain ribbon used as the center weft becomes
the bow on this easy woven tieback.*

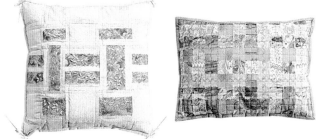

*Lavender 'n Lace by Mary Anne Caplinger,
1994, Wilkesboro, North Carolina, 16" x 16". Fancy
ribbons and trims accentuate the basic over-and-
under weaving pattern in this pillow top.*

*Peaches 'n Beads by Karen James Swing, 1994,
Boone, North Carolina, 14" x 14". Pearl beads, print
strips, and ribbon bows embellish pale peach and
ivory fabrics on this romantic pillow.*

*Mint 'n Metallic by Mary Anne Caplinger,
1994, Wilkesboro, North Carolina, 12 1/2" x 9 1/2".
Sparkling dew drops on silvery green leaves inspired
the color scheme for this pillow top. Gold metallic
threads highlight the soft green and neutral strips.*

*Garden Lap Robe by Mary Anne Caplinger,
1994, Wilkesboro, North Carolina, 33½" x 47½".
Widely spaced warp and weft strips form a lattice
that invites you to look beyond, into the garden.*

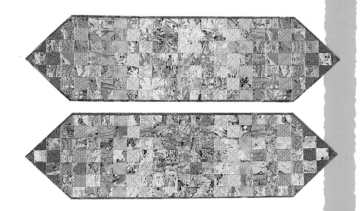

*Garden Table Runners by Mary Anne Caplinger,
1994, Wilkesboro, North Carolina, 10½" x 38".
Weft strips shift from dark purple to pale green
to purple again, reflecting the changing
colors of the garden.*

LAP ROBE

33½" x 47½"

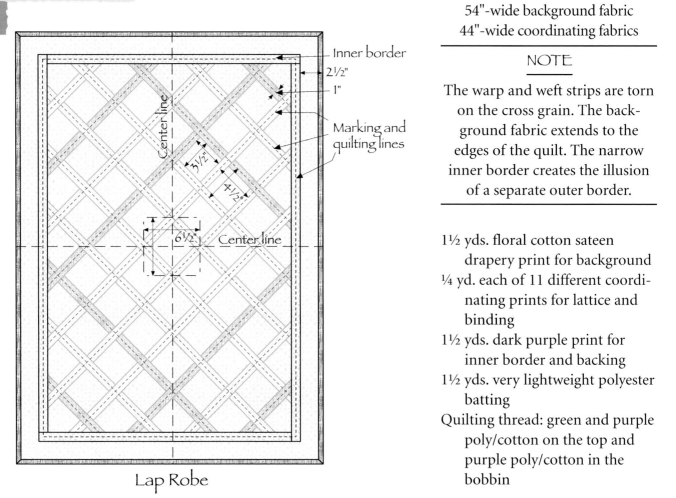

Lap Robe

MATERIALS

54"-wide background fabric
44"-wide coordinating fabrics

NOTE

The warp and weft strips are torn on the cross grain. The background fabric extends to the edges of the quilt. The narrow inner border creates the illusion of a separate outer border.

1½ yds. floral cotton sateen drapery print for background

¼ yd. each of 11 different coordinating prints for lattice and binding

1½ yds. dark purple print for inner border and backing

1½ yds. very lightweight polyester batting

Quilting thread: green and purple poly/cotton on the top and purple poly/cotton in the bobbin

Fabric	Used for	Number of Pieces	Size
Floral print	Background	1	35" x 49"
Coordinating prints	Binding	1	2½" x 180"**
	Warp	Varies*	1" wide
	Weft	Varies*	1" wide
Dark purple	Backing	1	35" x 49"
	Inner border	2	1" x 28½"
		2	1" x 42½"
Batting		1	35" x 49"

*Number and length of coordinating warp and weft strips will vary, depending on how you piece them.
**Piece the binding from various lengths of coordinating prints.

DIRECTIONS

For complete instructions, refer to "The Woven and Quilted Process," beginning on page 19.

Weaving

In this quilt, the warp and weft are spread on the background fabric. It doesn't matter which is considered the warp and which the weft; you will weave the strips as you would for any other piece. To keep your weaving straight, you'll lightly mark guidelines for the inner border and the warp and weft strips.

1. Fold the background fabric in half lengthwise and press; fold the fabric in half crosswise and press. Unfold and gently smooth the fabric. Using chalk and your rotary ruler or yardstick, mark the center lines.

2. Measure and mark the guidelines for the inner border as shown in the weaving diagram.

3. Using the 45° line on your rotary ruler and the center lines on the diagram, measure and mark the guidelines for the diagonal warp and weft strips. These guidelines are 4½" apart. The on-point squares that form are 6½" from point to point.

4. Secure the backing and batting to your work surface; see step 4 of "Getting Started" on page 20. Lay the marked background fabric on the batting and secure it.

5. Prepare the strips; see "Preparing Strips from a Full Width of Fabric" on page 23.

6. Lay the warp strips on the background fabric, centering the strips on the guidelines. Piece the strips as desired, making sure you overlap the ends at the intersections of the warp and weft guidelines. See "Changing Fabrics in the Middle of a Row" on page 27.

7. Weave the weft strips, piecing the strips as desired; see "Weaving the Weft Strips," page 24.

8. Pin-baste the layers, placing the pins every 1½"–2"; see "Pin Basting" on page 27.

Quilting

1. Quilt in the center of each warp and weft strip; see "Machine Quilting" on pages 27–28. Finish each row by bringing the bobbin thread to the top and tying the threads; clip the threads.

2. Lay the inner border strips over the guidelines and pin-baste. Quilt in the center of the strips.

Attaching the Binding

1. Trim the outer edges of the quilt to the finished size, 33½" x 47½".

2. Trim the ends of various 2½" binding pieces at a 45° angle and seam; press the seams open. Piece enough binding to make 180".

3. Attach the binding; see "Attaching the Binding" on pages 31–33. Disregard the references to the hanging sleeve.

LAVENDER 'N LACE

15½" x 15½"

Lavender 'n Lace

MATERIALS
44"-wide fabric

NOTE
The warp and weft strips are torn
on the cross grain.

⅛ yd. each of 6 coordinating purple print
fabrics for warp and weft
½ yd. purple print for pillow back
¼ yd. purple print for binding
½ yd. each of 12 different ribbons and trims, or
a combination of trims to equal 12 pieces,
each 16" long
½ yd. very lightweight polyester batting
Polyester fiberfill for stuffing
Quilting thread: purple, off-white, and green
rayon on the top and white poly/cotton in
the bobbin
See directions on pages 66–67.

Fabric	Used for	Number of Pieces	Size
Coordinating purple prints	Warp	7	1" x 16"
	Warp	3	1¼" x 16"
	Warp	3	1½" x 16"
	Weft	6	1" x 16"
	Weft	4	1¼" x 16"
	Weft	3	1½" x 16"
Purple print	Pillow back	1	16" x 16"
Purple print	Binding	1	2½" x 75"
Trims	Warp	7	16" lengths
	Weft	5	16" lengths
Batting		2	16" x 16"

PEACHES 'N BEADS

MATERIALS

44"-wide fabric

NOTE

The warp and weft strips are torn on the cross grain.

¾ yd. pale peach print for pillow back, warp, and binding

⅜ yd. off-white print for weft

⅛ yd. coordinating floral print for warp and weft

1 yd. peach ribbon, ⅛" wide

4 dozen (approximately) small pearl beads

½ yd. very lightweight polyester batting

Polyester fiberfill for stuffing

Quilting thread: peach poly/cotton on the top and white poly/cotton in the bobbin

See directions on pages 66–67.

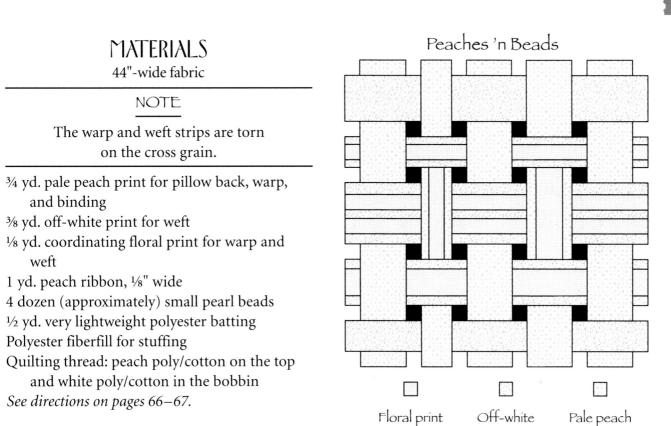

Peaches 'n Beads

Floral print (on top of off-white)   Off-white   Pale peach

Fabric	Used for	Number of Pieces	Size
Pale peach print	Pillow back	1	15" x 15"
	Warp	1	2" x 15"
	Warp	4	3" x 15"
	Binding	1	2" x 65"
Off-white print	Weft	2	2" x 15"
	Weft	2	3" x 15"
	Weft	1	4" x 15"
Floral print	Warp	1	1" x 15"
	Warp	1	1¾" x 15"
	Weft	3	1" x 15"
	Weft	1	1¾" x 15"
Ribbon	Bows	4	9" lengths
Batting		2	15" x 15"

MINT 'N METALLIC

12½" x 9½"

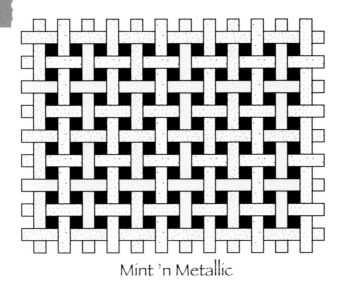

Mint 'n Metallic

MATERIALS
44"-wide fabric

NOTE

The warp and weft strips are torn
on the cross grain.

⅛ yd. each (or small pieces) of 7 coordinating
light green prints for warp and weft

½ yd. green print for pillow back and binding

⅜ yd. very lightweight polyester batting

Polyester fiberfill for stuffing

Quilting thread: green rayon, beige poly/cotton,
and gold metallic on the top and beige poly/
cotton in the bobbin

Fabric	Used for	Number of Pieces	Size
Coordinating prints	Warp	12	1" x 10"
	Weft	9	1" x 13"
Green print	Pillow back	1	10" x 13"
	Binding	1	1½" x 55"
Batting		2	10" x 13"

DIRECTIONS

For complete instructions, refer to "The
Woven and Quilted Process," beginning on page 19.

Weaving

You weave and quilt the pillow tops on the
batting without backing. If it's difficult for your
machine to sew with the batting on the machine
bed, slip a piece of tissue paper under the batting.
Remove the tissue paper after you finish quilting.

The weaving diagrams suggest the placement
of warp and weft strips. If you prefer, experiment
with your strips to find other pleasing arrangements.

1. Using pins or masking tape, secure the batting
and tissue paper, if needed, to your work surface.

2. Prepare the strips; see "Preparing Strips
from a Full Width of Fabric" on page 23. For
Lavender 'n Lace only, center lengths of ribbon
or trim on a variety of strips. Secure the trim
with a dot of fabric glue every inch.

3. Lay the warp strips on the batting in the order
shown in the weaving diagram of the pillow
you're making.

4. Weave the weft strips; see "Weaving the Weft
Strips" on page 24. Check the alignment every
other row, using your rotary ruler.

5. Pin-baste the layers; see "Pin Basting," page 27.

Quilting

Quilt in the center of each warp and weft strip; see "Machine Quilting" on pages 27–28. Use decorative machine stitches, if desired, to embellish the pillow tops.

For Lavender 'n Lace, avoid stitching over the heavy trims. The quilting in the adjacent rows will hold the trims in place.

Finishing

1. For Peaches 'n Beads, arrange the beads on the floral strips and sew by hand.

2. Trim the pillow top to the finished size.

3. You'll apply the mitered-corner binding to the pillow front and back as you would to a quilt. The first part of the binding is stitched to the pillow front only to allow for the opening.

   Begin at the bottom of the pillow, a few inches from the right corner. Fold the binding at a 45° angle as shown. With right sides together and raw edges aligned, stitch the binding to the lower edge to within a few inches of the opposite corner, using the proper seam allowance (½" for Lavender 'n Lace, ⅜" for Peaches 'n Beads, and ¼" for Mint 'n Metallic). Break the thread and take the pillow top from the machine.

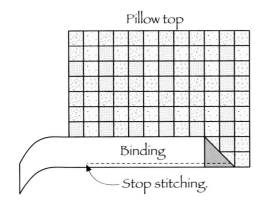

Pillow top

Binding

Stop stitching.

4. Place the pillow back face down on your work surface. Cover the back with the second piece of batting. Layer the pillow top, with the binding partially applied, on the batting and pillow back. Trim any excess batting or fabric at the edges of the pillow back.

5. Attach the binding; see "Attaching the Binding," step 4, on page 32 to form the mitered corners. Stitch on top of the previous stitching for 1"; continue around the pillow, stopping 1" beyond the folded end of the binding. You'll be left with an opening for inserting the fiberfill.

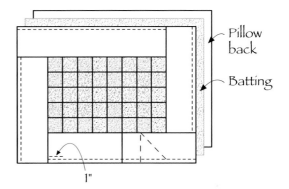

Pillow back

Batting

1"

6. Beginning at one edge of the opening, fold the binding to the back and turn under the raw edge so that the fold just covers the stitching; pin. Continue folding and pinning the binding until you reach the other edge of the opening. Slipstitch the binding to the back of the pillow. Stuff the pillow with fiberfill and slipstitch the opening closed.

7. For Peaches 'n Beads, sew a small bow in each corner.

TABLE RUNNER

10½" x 38"

Table Runner

MATERIALS

54"-wide theme fabric
44"-wide coordinating fabrics

NOTE

The coordinating fabrics are *torn* on the cross grain; the theme fabric is *cut* on the cross grain. The materials listed below are for two table runners; the directions are for one.

1 yd. floral print cotton sateen drapery fabric for warp and weft
⅛ yd. each of 10 different purple and green coordinating prints for weft
1 yd. dark purple print for backing and binding
Quilting thread: 2 or 3 coordinating colors of cotton/poly on the top and coordinating cotton/poly in the bobbin

Fabric	Used for	Number of Pieces	Size
Floral print	Warp	14	1½" x 40"
	Weft	10	1½" x 11"
Coordinating prints	Weft	36	1½" x 11"
Dark purple print	Backing	2	11" x 40"
	Binding	2	1¼" x 100

DIRECTIONS

For complete instructions, refer to "The Woven and Quilted Process," beginning on page 19.

Weaving

The batting is eliminated in the runners to allow them to drape softly over the ends of a table.

1. Using pins or masking tape, secure the backing fabric to the work surface.

2. Prepare the strips; see "Preparing Strips from a Full Width of Fabric" on page 23. Lay the warp strips on the backing as shown in the weaving diagram.

3. Weave the weft strips; see "Weaving the Weft Strips" on page 24. In the table runners shown on pages 60 and 61, the darker weft strips are placed at the tips of the runner and the lighter strips at the center.

Quilting

Create a grid by marking diagonal lines through the centers of the squares. Quilt the diagonal lines in one direction, then turn the piece and quilt the lines in the other direction; see "Machine Quilting" on pages 27–28.

Finishing

1. Trim the outer edges. Cut the ends on the diagonal.

2. Attach the binding; see "Attaching the Binding" on pages 31–33. When you come to the place where the long edge turns toward the end point, apply the binding as you would on a corner. Because the angle is wider, the diagonal fold will be smaller.

CURTAIN TIEBACK

MATERIALS
44"-wide fabric

NOTE

The warp and weft strips are torn on the cross grain.

2 yds. grosgrain ribbon, ¾" wide, for weft and bow

⅛ yd. each of 2 green prints for weft

⅛ yd. each (or small scraps) of coordinating green and purple prints for warp

¼ yd. dark purple print for backing and binding

⅛ yd. very lightweight polyester batting

Quilting thread: green poly/cotton on the top and dark purple poly/cotton in the bobbin

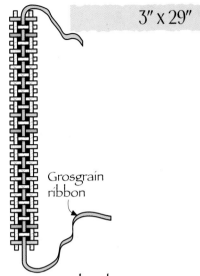

3" x 29"

Grosgrain ribbon

Curtain Tieback

Fabric	Used for	Number of Pieces	Size
Grosgrain ribbon	Weft and bow	1	72" length
Green prints	Weft	2	1" x 30"
Coordinating prints	Warp	29	1" x 3"
Purple print	Backing	1	3½" x 30"
	Binding	1	1½" x 70"
Batting		1	3½" x 30"

DIRECTIONS

For complete instructions, refer to "The Woven and Quilted Process," beginning on page 19.

Weaving

1. Secure the backing and batting to your work surface; see step 4 of "Getting Started," page 20.

2. Prepare the strips; see "Preparing Strips from a Full Width of Fabric" on page 23. Because the warp strips are so short compared to the weft strips, it's easiest to lay the weft strips first. The grosgrain ribbon, the center weft strip, extends beyond the ends and becomes the bow.

Find the center of the ribbon and place it on the center of the batting. Lay one green weft strip on either side of the ribbon.

3. Weave the short warp strips as you would weft strips; see "Weaving the Weft Strips," page 24.

4. Pin-baste; see "Pin Basting" on page 27.

Quilting

Quilt in the center of each warp and weft strip. On the ribbon, start and stop stitching 1" from each end; see "Machine Quilting" on pages 27–28.

Finishing

1. Fold the ends of the ribbon toward the center and pin them out of the way. Trim the tieback to the finished size, 3" x 29".

2. Attach the binding using a ¼"-wide seam allowance; see "Attaching the Binding" on pages 31–33. Be careful not to catch the ribbon in the binding.

3. Unpin the ribbon ends and press the tieback lightly. Loop the tieback around the curtain and tie the ribbon in a bow.

Good Morning! by Mary Anne Caplinger, 1994, Wilkesboro, North Carolina.
Sunny curtains and a tailored valance brighten any kitchen setting. Woven and quilted
place mats, napkin rings, and a centerpiece coordinate with the window treatment.

A simple woven border at the curtain hem echoes the weaving pattern of the valance and place mats.

Layered buttons hold each miniquilt on the decorative rod.

A small miniquilt, folded and "buttoned," makes a novel napkin ring.

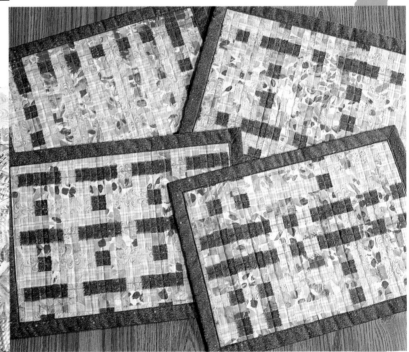

The arrangement of warp and weft strips changes from place mat to place mat, creating a varied, yet coordinated, set.

VALANCE

Each section of this valance is a reversible miniquilt that's folded, "buttoned," and draped over a decorative curtain rod. The yardages and directions that follow are for one miniquilt. The photo on page 70 shows four miniquilts on a double window; make the number you need to cover your curtain rod. You can also use the miniquilt as a trivet for the center of a table—just eliminate the buttons.

Valance and Trivet

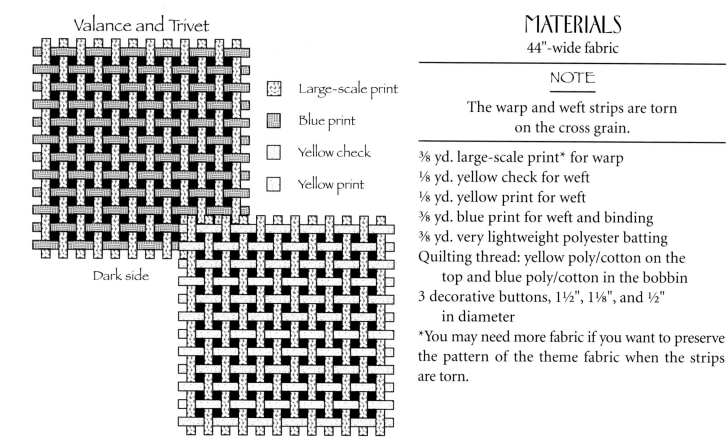

Dark side

Light side

⊞ Large-scale print

▦ Blue print

☐ Yellow check

☐ Yellow print

MATERIALS
44"-wide fabric

NOTE
The warp and weft strips are torn on the cross grain.

⅜ yd. large-scale print* for warp
⅛ yd. yellow check for weft
⅛ yd. yellow print for weft
⅜ yd. blue print for weft and binding
⅜ yd. very lightweight polyester batting
Quilting thread: yellow poly/cotton on the top and blue poly/cotton in the bobbin
3 decorative buttons, 1½", 1⅛", and ½" in diameter

*You may need more fabric if you want to preserve the pattern of the theme fabric when the strips are torn.

Fabric	Used for	Number of Pieces	Size
Large-scale print	Warp	24	1" x 12"
Yellow check	Weft	8	1" x 12"
Yellow print	Weft	4	1" x 12"
Blue print	Weft	12	1" x 12"
	Binding	1	2⅛" x 60"
Batting		2	12" x 12"

DIRECTIONS

For complete instructions, refer to "The Woven and Quilted Process," beginning on page 19.

Weaving

The reversible miniquilt consists of two woven and quilted pieces joined at the edges with binding. The extra layers of fabric and batting create a piece that hangs straight when draped over a curtain rod. Because the two pieces are placed back to back, there's no need for a backing.

In the miniquilts shown here, the warp strips are arranged randomly, creating scattered red accents.

1. Using pins or masking tape, secure a piece of batting to your work surface.

2. Prepare the strips; see "Preparing Strips from a Full Width of Fabric" on page 23.

3. Lay the warp strips on the batting in the order shown in the weaving diagram.

4. Weave the yellow check and yellow print weft strips; see "Weaving the Weft Strips" on page 24. Check the alignment every other row using your rotary ruler.

5. Pin-baste; see "Pin Basting" on page 27.

6. Weave and pin-baste the second piece, using the blue weft strips.

Quilting

If it's difficult for your machine to sew with the batting on the machine bed, slip a piece of tissue paper under the batting. Remove the tissue paper after you finish quilting.

On the first woven piece, quilt in the center of each warp and weft strip, using the yellow thread on top. Quilt the second piece, using the blue thread on top. See "Machine Quilting" on pages 27–28.

Finishing

1. Trim each quilted piece to the finished size, 12" x 12". Layer the two pieces, wrong sides together, and pin the edges.

2. Attach the binding; see "Attaching the Binding" on pages 31–33.

3. Drape the finished miniquilt over the rod and mark the button placement. Remove the quilt and sew on the buttons.

CAFE CURTAINS

Custom

Simple cafe curtains feature a woven border that coordinates with the valance. The curtains shown on pages 70 and 71 consist of four separate panels, each made from one width of fabric.

To determine the yardage needed, measure ready-made curtains that fit your window, including the fabric in the heading and hems.

Or follow these steps to calculate the yardage:

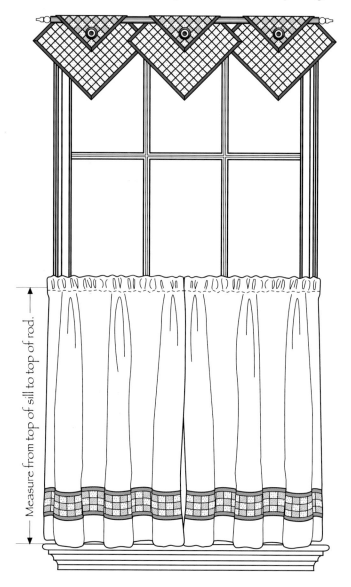

Measure from top of sill to top of rod.

1. Measure the length of your window from the top of the curtain rod to the window sill as shown. Add 7½" for the top allowance, 6" for the lower hem, and 1" to square the ends. Also add ½" take-up allowance for a flat rod or, for a round rod, the diameter of the rod. The sum is the cut length.

2. Decide how many curtain panels (widths) you need. For standard fullness, the total width of all the panels should be approximately 2½ times the window width.

3. Multiply the cut length by the number of panels for the total inches of fabric required. Divide this total by 36" for the yards needed.

4. Measure and cut the length needed for each panel. Trim the panel slightly, if necessary, to make the width measurement a whole number.

As an example, following are the yardages for four panels:

MATERIALS
44"-wide fabric

NOTE

The warp and weft strips are torn on the cross grain.

5½ yds. yellow check for curtain panels
½ yd. large-scale print for weft
½ yd. yellow print for warp
¼ yd. blue print for border
Quilting thread: white poly/cotton

Fabric	Used for	No. of Pieces	Size
Yellow check	Curtains	No. of panels	Cut length*
Large-scale print	Weft	No. of panels x 3	1" x cut panel width
Yellow print	Warp	No. = to finished panel width	1" x 3¾"
Blue print	Border	No. of panels x 2	¾" x cut panel width

*Varies, depending on your window size.

DIRECTIONS

For complete instructions, refer to "The Woven and Quilted Process," beginning on page 19.

Making the Curtains

1. To make the side hems, turn in each edge 1", wrong sides together, and press. Turn in another 1" and press. Pin-baste and stitch close to the edge of the first fold.

2. Repeat on the lower hem, turning up and pressing 3" twice. The stitching will be covered by the narrow borders.

Weaving

Because the warp strips are so short compared to the weft, it's easiest to lay the long weft strips first.

1. Lay the first weft strip at the lower edge, just above the hem stitching. Make sure the strip is centered widthwise; 2" should extend beyond each side hem.

2. At each side, fold under 1" and wrap the strip so the folded end meets the edge of the side hem. Pin the weft strip. Lay the second weft strip above the first one and wrap the ends in the same way. Repeat for the third weft strip.

3. Weave the 3¾" warp strips, beginning and ending even with the sides of the curtain; you may need to adjust the spacing of the strips toward the center. The warp strips will extend slightly above and below the weft to allow them to be caught in the stitching when you apply the borders. Check the alignment of the strips, using your rotary ruler or yardsticks.

4. Pin-baste the layers; see "Pin Basting," page 27.

Quilting

1. Stitch in the center of each weft strip; see "Machine Quilting" on pages 27–28. If you anticipate washing the curtains often, also stitch in the center of each warp strip.

2. Lay a border strip on the upper and lower edges of the weaving and pin. Wrap the ends as you did on the long weft strips. Stitch in the center of each border.

Finishing

To make the rod pocket at the top of the curtain, fold 3" down, wrong sides together, and press. Fold down another 3" and press. Pin-baste and stitch close to the edge of the first fold. To create the heading, stitch 1½" from the top fold.

PLACE MATS

18" x 13"

Each place mat in this set of four has a slightly different look because the arrangement of the warp and weft strips varies. The materials listed below are for four place mats; the directions are for one.

The backing and border consist of one piece. You weave and quilt the place mat first, then fold mitered corners on the backing to form the borders. The place mat slips under the border, which is then topstitched.

Place mat

| Large-scale print | Blue print | Yellow check | Yellow print |

MATERIALS
44"-wide fabric

NOTE

The warp and weft strips are torn on the cross grain.

⅝ yd. large-scale print for warp and weft

½ yd. yellow check for warp and weft

½ yd. yellow print for warp and weft

2½ yds. blue print for warp, weft, and backing

1½ yds. heavyweight fusible interfacing, 20" wide

Quilting thread: yellow poly/cotton on the top and blue poly/cotton in the bobbin

Fabric	Used for	Number of Pieces	Size
Large-scale print	Warp	Varies*	1" x 13"
	Weft	Varies	1" x 18"
Yellow check	Warp	Varies	1" x 13"
	Weft	Varies	1" x 18"
Yellow print	Warp	Varies	1" x 13"
	Weft	Varies	1" x 18"
Blue print	Warp	Varies	1" x 13"
	Weft	Varies	1" x 18"
	Backing	4	17" x 22"
Fusible interfacing	Underlining	4	17" x 22"

*For 4 place mats, tear or cut from each fabric approximately 20 warp strips and 15 weft strips.

DIRECTIONS

For complete instructions, refer to "The Woven and Quilted Process," beginning on page 19.

Weaving

1. Secure one piece of batting to your work surface, using pins or masking tape.

2. Prepare the strips; see "Preparing Strips from a Full Width of Fabric" on page 23. Lay the warp strips on the batting as shown in the weaving diagram. On the other place mats, experiment with the arrangement of the strips to achieve different effects.

3. Weave the weft strips; see "Weaving the Weft Strips" on page 24. Check the alignment of the strips using your rotary ruler or yardsticks.

4. Pin-baste the layers; see "Pin Basting," page 27.

Quilting

You quilt the woven piece without a backing. If it's difficult for your machine to sew with the batting on the machine bed, slip a piece of tissue paper under the batting. Remove the tissue paper after you finish quilting.

Quilt in the center of each warp and weft strip or quilt a pattern of your choice; see "Machine Quilting" on pages 27–28. To enhance the surface design, alternate the yellow and blue thread on the top.

Constructing the Borders

Making the mitered-corner border takes a little practice; try this technique on a scrap of fabric before you work on your place mat. It's not difficult, but you do need to measure accurately.

1. Trim the quilted piece to 17½" x 12½".

2. Fuse the interfacing to the wrong side of the backing according to the manufacturer's instructions.

3. Lay the backing, interfaced side up, on your pressing surface. At the upper edge, fold ¾" toward the center and press a sharp crease. Make a second fold, 1¼" deep; press a sharp crease. Undo these folds and gently smooth them

without losing the creases. Rotate the backing and press two folds on each remaining edge.

4. Refold the first ¾" crease on the upper and the right edge, keeping it open at the corner. Hold the upper edge in your left hand about 3" from the right corner. Hold the right edge in your right hand about 3" from the corner. Bring the right sides of the back together and match the creased edges to form a triangle.

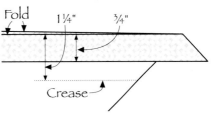

5. Lay the piece on your work surface with the folded edges up and the diagonal fold to the lower right. Along the upper edges, measure 2½" from the corner and mark. Along the diagonal interfaced fold, measure 1¾" and mark. This mark should fall at the intersection of the second folds; you should be able to see the creases.

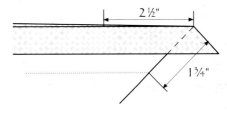

6. Connect the two marks with a straight line; stitch on the line.

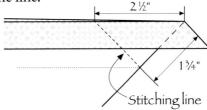

7. Trim the point, leaving a ½"-wide seam allowance. Open the seam allowance and finger-press. Turn the border right side out and admire your mitered corner! Repeat for the other three corners.

8. Lift the border and gently insert the woven and quilted top, centering it in the border "frame." Pin-baste the layers around the border. Topstitch ⅛" from the inner edge of the border.

NAPKIN RINGS

6" x 6", flat

Each napkin ring is a miniquilt folded into a triangle and secured with a button. The materials listed below are for four napkin rings; the directions are for one.

Napkin Ring

☷ Large-scale print

▦ Blue print

MATERIALS
44"-wide fabric

NOTE

The warp and weft strips are torn on the cross grain.

⅜ yd. blue print for warp and binding
¼ yd. large-scale print for weft
¼ yd. yellow check for backing
¼ yd. very lightweight polyester batting
Quilting thread: blue poly/cotton on the top
    and yellow poly/cotton in the bobbin
4 decorative buttons
1 yd. blue print for matching napkins

Fabric	Used for	Number of Pieces	Size
Blue print	Warp	6	1" x 6½"
	Binding	1	1¼" x 33"
Large-scale print	Weft	6	1" x 6½"
Yellow check	Backing	1	6½" x 6½"
Batting		1	6½" x 6½"

DIRECTIONS

For complete instructions, refer to "The Woven and Quilted Process," beginning on page 19.

Weaving

1. Secure the batting and backing to your work surface; see step 4 of "Getting Started," page 20.

2. Prepare the strips; see "Preparing Strips from a Full Width of Fabric" on page 23. Lay the warp strips on the batting as shown in the weaving diagram.

3. Weave the weft strips; see "Weaving the Weft Strips" on page 24.

4. Check the alignment, using your rotary ruler.

5. Pin-baste the layers; see "Pin Basting," page 27.

Quilting

Quilt in the center of each warp and weft strip; see "Machine Quilting" on pages 27–28.

Finishing

1. Lightly press the woven and quilted piece and trim to the finished size, 6" x 6". Apply the binding, using a ¼"-wide seam allowance; see "Attaching the Binding" on pages 31–33.

2. Fold the finished miniquilt on the diagonal. Sew on a button to hold the corners.

3. For matching napkins, tear the fabric into 17" squares. Remove the ravels and press. Sew with a straight or decorative stitch 1" from the edges.

RESOURCES

Collapsible Cardboard Cutting Table
    Sew/Fit Company
    PO Box 565
    LaGrange, IL 60525

Work Space Board
    Keepsake Quilting
    Route 25
    PO Box 1618
    Centre Harbor, NH 03226-1618
    603/253-8731

Poppanna
    Eaton Yarns
    PO Box 665
    Tarrytown, NY 10591
    914/631-1550

MACHINE QUILTING BOOKS

Fanning, Robbie and Tony Fanning. *The Complete Book of Machine Quilting.* Radnor, Pa.: Chilton Book Company, 1980.

Hargrave, Harriet. *Heirloom Machine Quilting.* Lafayette, Calif.: C & T Publishing, 1990.

Noble, Maurine. *Machine Quilting Made Easy.* Bothell, Wash.: That Patchwork Place, 1994.

Smith, Lois. *Easy Machine Quilting.* Paducah, Ky.: American Quilter's Society, 1990.

MEET THE AUTHOR

Mary Anne's love of fiber and fabric processes was a heritage passed down from her mother and grandmothers. "As soon as my mother felt comfortable with it, I had a needle in my hand," she says. "According to her, my second word was 'scissors.'"

Over the years, as she realized the creative possibilities inherent in cloth, Mary Anne began experimenting with a variety of textile structures and surface-design techniques. Today, she devotes her time and creative energies to fabric painting, dyeing, silk-screen printing, and stamping. She dyes by hand almost all the fabrics she uses in her weaving.

Mary Anne has been making and exhibiting quilts and quilted wearables since 1973. As a balance to the long hours spent working alone, she enjoys teaching quilting and surface design to quilters in the Southeast. When she's not working with fabric, Mary Anne likes to read, garden, and travel.

Native midwesterners, Mary Anne and her husband, John, now live in Wilkesboro, North Carolina, where they are both active in the local community. They are the parents of two grown children.

That Patchwork Place Publications and Products

All the Blocks Are Geese
    by Mary Sue Suit
Angle Antics by Mary Hickey
Animas Quilts by Jackie Robinson
Appliqué Borders: An Added Grace
    by Jeana Kimball
Appliqué in Bloom by Gabrielle Swain
Appliquilt: Whimsical One-Step Appliqué
    by Tonee White
Around the Block with Judy Hopkins
Baltimore Bouquets by Mimi Dietrich
Bargello Quilts by Marge Edie
Basket Garden by Mary Hickey
Biblical Blocks by Rosemary Makhan
Blockbuster Quilts by Margaret J. Miller
Borders by Design by Paulette Peters
Botanical Wreaths by Laura M. Reinstatler
Calendar Quilts by Joan Hanson
Cathedral Window: A Fresh Look
    by Nancy J. Martin
The Cat's Meow by Janet Kime
A Child's Garden of Quilts
    by Christal Carter
Colourwash Quilts by Deirdre Amsden
Corners in the Cabin by Paulette Peters
Country Medallion Sampler
    by Carol Doak
Country Threads by Connie Tesene and
    Mary Tendall
Decoupage Quilts by Barbara Roberts
Designing Quilts by Suzanne Hammond
The Easy Art of Appliqué
    by Mimi Dietrich & Roxi Eppler
Easy Machine Paper Piecing
    by Carol Doak
Easy Quilts...By Jupiter!®
    by Mary Beth Maison
Easy Reversible Vests by Carol Doak
Fantasy Flowers
    by Doreen Cronkite Burbank
Five- and Seven-Patch Blocks & Quilts for
    the ScrapSaver by Judy Hopkins
Four-Patch Blocks & Quilts for the
    ScrapSaver by Judy Hopkins
Fun with Fat Quarters by Nancy J. Martin
Go Wild with Quilts by Margaret Rolfe
Handmade Quilts by Mimi Dietrich
Happy Endings by Mimi Dietrich
The Heirloom Quilt by Yolande Filson
    and Roberta Przybylski

Holiday Happenings by Christal Carter
In The Beginning by Sharon Evans Yenter
Irma's Sampler by Irma Eskes
Jacket Jazz by Judy Murrah
Jacket Jazz Encore by Judy Murrah
Le Rouvray by Diane de Obaldia,
    with Marie-Christine Flocard and
    Cosabeth Parriaud
Lessons in Machine Piecing
    by Marsha McCloskey
Little Quilts by Alice Berg, Sylvia Johnson,
    and Mary Ellen Von Holt
Lively Little Logs by Donna McConnell
Loving Stitches by Jeana Kimball
Machine Quilting Made Easy
    by Maurine Noble
Make Room for Quilts by Nancy J. Martin
Nifty Ninepatches by Carolann M. Palmer
Nine-Patch Blocks & Quilts for the
    ScrapSaver by Judy Hopkins
Not Just Quilts by Jo Parrott
Oh! Christmas Trees
    compiled by Barbara Weiland
On to Square Two by Marsha McCloskey
Osage County Quilt Factory
    by Virginia Robertson
Our Pieceful Village by Lynn Rice
Painless Borders by Sally Schneider
A Perfect Match by Donna Lynn Thomas
Picture Perfect Patchwork
    by Naomi Norman
Piecemakers® Country Store
    by the Piecemakers
Pineapple Passion
    by Nancy Smith and Lynda Milligan
A Pioneer Doll and Her Quilts
    by Mary Hickey
Pioneer Storybook Quilts by Mary Hickey
Prairie People—Cloth Dolls to Make
    and Cherish by Marji Hadley and
    J. Dianne Ridgley
Quick & Easy Quiltmaking by Mary Hickey,
    Nancy J. Martin, Marsha McCloskey
    and Sara Nephew
The Quilted Apple by Laurene Sinema
Quilted for Christmas
    compiled by Ursula Reikes
The Quilters' Companion
    compiled by That Patchwork Place

The Quilting Bee
    by Jackie Wolff and Lori Aluna
Quilting Makes the Quilt by Lee Cleland
Quilts for All Seasons by Christal Carter
Quilts for Baby: Easy as A, B, C
    by Ursula Reikes
Quilts for Kids by Carolann M. Palmer
Quilts from Nature by Joan Colvin
Quilts to Share by Janet Kime
Red Wagon Originals
    by Gerry Kimmel and Linda Brannock
Rotary Riot
    by Judy Hopkins and Nancy J. Martin
Rotary Roundup
    by Judy Hopkins and Nancy J. Martin
Round About Quilts by J. Michelle Watts
Round Robin Quilts
    by Pat Magaret and Donna Slusser
Samplings from the Sea
    by Rosemary Makhan
ScrapMania by Sally Schneider
Seasoned with Quilts by Retta Warehime
Sensational Settings by Joan Hanson
Sewing on the Line
    by Lesly-Claire Greenberg
Shortcuts: A Concise Guide to Rotary
    Cutting by Donna Lynn Thomas
Shortcuts Sampler by Roxanne Carter
Shortcuts to the Top
    by Donna Lynn Thomas
Small Talk by Donna Lynn Thomas
Smoothstitch® Quilts by Roxi Eppler
The Stitchin' Post
    by Jean Wells and Lawry Thorn
Stringing Along by Trice Boerens
Strips That Sizzle by Margaret J. Miller
Sunbonnet Sue All Through the Year
    by Sue Linker
Tea Party Time by Nancy J. Martin
Template-Free® Quiltmaking
    by Trudie Hughes
Template-Free® Quilts and Borders
    by Trudie Hughes
Template-Free® Stars by Jo Parrott
Treasures from Yesteryear: Book One
    by Sharon Newman
Two for Your Money by Jo Parrott
Watercolor Quilts
    by Pat Magaret and Donna Slusser
Woven & Quilted by Mary Anne Caplinger

4", 6", 8", & metric Bias Square® • BiRangle™ • Ruby Beholder™ • Pineapple Rule • ScrapMaster • Rotary Rule™ • Rotary Mate™
Shortcuts to America's Best-Loved Quilts (video)

Many titles are available at your local quilt shop. For more information, send $2 for a
color catalog to That Patchwork Place, Inc., PO Box 118, Bothell WA 98041-0118 USA.

☎ Call 1-800-426-3126 for the name and location of the quilt shop nearest you.